GIFTED
EDUCATION
Promising
Practices

Joan Franklin Smutny

PHI DELTA KAPPA
EDUCATIONAL FOUNDATION
Bloomington, Indiana
U.S.A.

Cover design by
Victoria Voelker

Phi Delta Kappa Educational Foundation
408 North Union Street
Post Office Box 789
Bloomington, IN 47402-0789
U.S.A.

Printed in the United States of America

Library of Congress Control Number 2003100181
ISBN 0-87367-845-1
Copyright 2003 by Joan Franklin Smutny

To the thousands of teachers, counselors,
administrators, and college educators
who see the promise of gifted children
and who desire to advance their lives
so that they may contribute,
perceptively and creatively,
to humankind.

TABLE OF CONTENTS

ACKNOWLEDGEMENTS

I gratefully acknowledge the following colleagues whose support and vision have been a constant source of inspiration: E. Paul Torrance, Barbara Clark, Sandy Berger, Jerry Flack, Dorothy Knopper, Margaret Gosfield, and Maurice Fischer.

I also appreciate the support of Donovan Walling of Phi Delta Kappa International, whose encouragement and insights on the writing of this book were invaluable.

INTRODUCTION

by Sandra L. Berger

Joan Franklin Smutny is a gift to gifted education. A consummate advocate, she is knowledgeable, eloquent, passionate, and dedicated to each child — those easy to spot as gifted and those who hide their gifts and are underserved. Her love for children is reflected on every page of this remarkable book.

The need for a book that pulls together all of the elements of gifted education programming has been evident for several years. From start to finish, *Gifted Education: Promising Practices* fulfills that need. A book for teachers, administrators, parents, students, and all who care about children, it is for the uninitiated as well as for those with expertise, clearly explaining the need for gifted education and the how-to's.

In Chapter One, Joan briefly traces the history of gifted education and the people who influenced the field of ability testing, describing how they set the stage for theories of intelligence and, by extension, set the agenda for gifted education. She also discusses challenges to the monolithic view of intelligence that shaped education during the early 20th century. Joan's deep connection to gifted child education and its historical context springs to life under her skilled pen as she explains how cognitive and developmental psychology led to current thinking about giftedness by describing the delicate balance between nature and nurture.

Chapter Two is concerned with the options open to educators responsible for matching the strengths and needs of children with program services, particularly how to recognize practical problems and potential loss of talent. New methods of objective and subjective assessment and identification have been developed to bring out the strengths of each child. Joan reviews the research and presents a variety of theories that, like colorful fibers blended together, create a rich intellectual tapestry.

The full range of elementary and secondary gifted education program options is presented in Chapters Three and Four. Readers can select an approach to serve an immediate need and later return for a more substantive reading. Joan concentrates on how to understand the nature of the classroom experience from a child's point of view and then to develop a repertoire of practices that encourage play, exploration, taking risks, and creatively solving problems. Advantages and disadvantages of pull-out, cluster, acceleration, and special classes provide a continuum for educator practice in the heterogeneous classroom with a variety of strategies that will enrich all children while providing gifted children with the means to work at a level of challenge.

In Chapter Five, on creativity, Joan demonstrates her passionate belief that "creativity is not simply a gift or ability, but underlies the very nature of some children. It determines how life is experienced, how problems are perceived, and how visions are realized." She writes as both an expert and a participant as she explains methods for fostering creativity.

Gifted girls, the focus of Chapter Six, are singled out in order to examine the challenges faced by young gifted women in today's schools. Joan's process for discovering talents in girls and then nurturing those talents is described, with emphasis on the powerful role mentors play.

In Chapter Seven, Joan offers fresh ideas for addressing a problem that has concerned educators for decades: the underrepresentation of minorities in gifted education. Students from low-income families in particular are woefully underrepresented in classes for high-ability students. Joan explains the issues and the steps necessary for successful programs.

The focus of Chapter Eight is underachievement. Joan dispels the myth that "underachieving gifted" is an oxymoron by exploring the factors involved in underachievement. She describes the characteristics that define gifted underachieving, exploring the causes as well as promising approaches and effective strategies to resolve the problem.

Finally, in Chapters Nine and Ten, Joan tackles program planning and evaluation. In so doing, she provides practitioners with the essential how-to's of effective gifted education programming.

So much has happened in gifted education in the past few years that undertaking a book on promising practices requires a sense of history and purpose, keen analytical ability, and creative imagination. Joan Smutny possesses all of these characteristics and puts them to good use in this valuable guide.

Sandra L. Berger is an information specialist in gifted education at the ERIC Clearinghouse on Disabilities and Gifted Education in Arlington, Virginia.

CHAPTER ONE

Historical Perspectives

Throughout history, societies have selected the most talented individuals for special tutoring and education. For example, during the Tang Dynasty (618-905), which was known for its encouragement of the arts and literature, China sent its gifted children to the Imperial Court where they could receive an education appropriate to their abilities. European governments during the Renaissance supported gifted individuals in art, architecture, and literature with wealth and honor (Davis and Rimm 1994). However, the term *gifted*, at least in the Western world, often signified a particular talent — Renoir was a "gifted artist," Mozart a "gifted musician," Emily Brontë a "gifted writer," and so on. It wasn't until the 20th century that the term *gifted* came to be used in a more general sense and so was applied to children who evidenced unusual abilities.

"Nature" Versus "Nurture"

Since the beginning of the 20th century, debates about the nature of giftedness have focused on a fundamental question:

Does a person's intelligence result primarily from hereditary ("nature") or environmental factors ("nurture")? Many intelligence theorists applied Charles Darwin's ideas about the "survival of the fittest" to this debate. For example, Sir Francis Galton, a cousin of Darwin, wrote a book called *Hereditary Genius* in 1869 — an extensive study of the eminent men of his time — and concluded that heredity determines an individual's intelligence more than any other factor. This view, in fact, dominated the field of education for many years.

About a century later, the first researcher to challenge this view in any significant way was a French psychologist, Alfred Binet (1969), who believed that intelligence was "educable." Known best for the scale, or test, he developed to distinguish "normal" from "dull" students in Parisian schools, Binet conceived of intelligence as the use of mental functions, such as attention, memory, discrimination, and practical judgment (Fancher 1985). By experimenting with his own children, Binet determined the "mental age" at which most children accomplish certain tasks. He then compared the responses of an unknown test subject with his scale and determined whether the subject was normal or below the average range of human intelligence. His purpose in so doing was to help the lower students raise their "mental age" through appropriate education or training.

Ironically, the very test Binet developed as an aid to improving the intelligence of low-performing students became the basis of the most widely accepted theory of hereditary and fixed intelligence in the 20th century. Lewis Terman, influenced by the theories of Sir Francis Galton, acquired English translations of Binet's scales at Stanford University and adapted them for a new purpose. He altered the tasks to suit American subjects and named the new scale the Stanford Revision of the Binet Scale (which became the Stanford-Binet Intelligence Test). He also practiced a new method of scoring, which involved calculating the ratio between mental and chronological age and multiplying by 100. The result was the Intelligence Quotient, a fixed and unitary quantity that, even today, claims to be a scientific measurement of intelligence. So respected was Terman's intelligence test that when other tests were developed, they were most often validated by correlating them with the Stanford-Binet.

Terman's interest in human intelligence also took another form: his longitudinal studies of gifted children. Based on his norming research, he had already identified 130 and above as a mark of "giftedness" and any number above 150 as "genius." (Feldman 1979). Terman and his associates then tested California schoolchildren to find a sample of 1,500 boys and girls with IQs above 140. They followed the lives of these subjects from the 1920s through 1955, and then Terman's associates continued the work through 1972. This longitudinal study provided a great deal of information about how intellectually precocious children become eminent; about how parents influence their interests, choices, and emotional well-being; and how an accelerated and enriched education fosters greater achievement. Terman also dispelled popular stereotypes that characterized gifted people as weak, sickly, abnormal, or mentally unstable. The main limitation of this study was the sample itself: All of the children were from middle-class white families. This fact later led researchers to consider the effects of cultural and socioeconomic bias on Terman's conclusions about intelligence and giftedness.

Challenges to Single-Score Intelligence

Over time a number of researchers have challenged the notion of single-score intelligence. Following are a few brief summaries of the most prominent of these challenges.

Primary Mental Abilities. In the 1930s, a University of Chicago psychologist, L.L. Thurstone, challenged the single-score concept of intelligence. While accepting that the IQ score might predict verbal academic achievement, Thurstone believed that it failed to predict success in other, less verbal, less academic endeavors. He theorized intelligence as seven "primary mental abilities," which he termed: verbal comprehension, word fluency, number facility, spatial visualization, associative memory, perceptual speed, and reasoning. He believed that Terman's composite score overlooked these independent aspects of intelligence (Thurstone 1938; Thurstone and Thurstone 1954).

Structure of the Intellect. California psychologist J.P. Guilford expanded on Thurstone's ideas and described a three-dimensional "structure of the intellect" model of intelligence that consists of 120 separate elements, or basic factors of intelligence. Guilford's research led him to conclude that intelligence in an individual is uneven and shows a range of strengths and weaknesses rather than one general ability level in all areas (as the single-score IQ implies). Using the research method of factor analysis, which was unknown to Terman and Thurstone, he differentiated and classified 80 distinct factors of intelligence and further predicted that 120 factors could be accounted for by his structure of the intellect (SOI) theory (Guilford 1967). Guilford's Structure of the Intellect Test is difficult to administer, score, and interpret. Yet his work clearly demonstrated the complex nature of the human intellect and questioned the reliability of the Stanford-Binet as a measurement of intelligence as a quantifiable element.

Cultural Bias. Other challenges to single-score intelligence came from those who felt that cultural bias had played a role in the theory of hereditary intelligence. The studies of Lewis Terman supported the sentiments and beliefs of zealous eugenicists who sought to prove the racial superiority of the "Nordic" races. "The whole question of racial differences in mental traits," Terman wrote, "will have to be taken up anew. . . . The writer predicts that when this is done there will be discovered enormously significant racial differences in general intelligence" (in Kamin 1974, p. 6). The innovative research of scholars such as E.M. Bernal (1981) claimed that identifying giftedness within other cultures should not be undertaken without consulting the definitions of talent and ability that prevail in these cultures. Cultural values tend to determine, to a large extent, the kinds of talents that bright people express.

U.S. Definition. In 1972, the U.S. Office of Education formally recognized the complexity of giftedness through a definition that included potential and achievement in the several areas (see Marland 1972, p. x). These areas include:

- General intellectual ability,
- Specific academic aptitude,
- Creative or productive thinking,
- Leadership ability,
- Visual and performing arts, and
- Psychomotor ability.

This federal definition reflected the growing perception that giftedness meant not only high general intelligence but also talent in academic areas and the arts, as well as in more generalizable areas such as creativity and leadership. In 1978 and 1988, this definition was revised to exclude the psychomotor gifts. Children gifted in sports could enter the school athletics programs, while those with talent in dance or mime would, ideally, be recognized by the visual and performing arts category of the definition.

A New Paradigm of Intelligence. In spite of the 1972 federal definition of giftedness, many school districts still adhered to the narrow concept of intelligence established by Terman, and they continued to use testing as the most reliable measure of ability. Alternatives, such as those of Guilford, seemed too complex to execute. But in the 1980s Howard Gardner (1983) at Harvard University and Robert Sternberg (1984) at Yale University helped to create a new paradigm for understanding intelligence. Although their work did not focus exclusively on giftedness, it provided a language for talking about the multifaceted nature of intelligence and how it functions in a variety of domains. Their views not only fostered the recognition of ability in many new areas but also provided a theoretical and conceptual framework for understanding how ability in these areas might manifest itself.

In Gardner's view — termed "multiple intelligences" — a number of relatively autonomous "intelligences" exist, each with its own language, symbols, and processes (Gardner 1983). *Linguistic intelligence* involves a sensitivity to oral and written language and may express itself through listening to speech, reading, writing, and interpreting text. *Musical intelligence* responds to sound, rhythm, harmony, and melody and may involve a keen sense of pitch; it often results in the composition and performance of music. *Logical-mathematical intelligence* excels in logic activities where the exercise of reason and the application of principles can achieve solutions to problems. *Spatial intelligence* demands visual-spatial acuity and results in contributions to art as well as to science in fields that require accurate visual memories of projections. *Bodily-kinesthetic intelligence* uses body movement to learn, solve problems, plan, and reason. Performing, playing sports, and constructing are examples. Gardner also includes *intrapersonal intelligence,* which means a high degree of self-knowledge and understanding, and *interpersonal intelligence,* which refers to an ability to understand, lead, and empathize with others.

Sternberg's triarchic definition of intelligence grew out of his background and interest in cognition, particularly information processing. He believed that previous theories of intelligence failed to explain the interaction between an individual and the real world. He criticized attempts to describe and assess intelligent behavior in terms of a response to an item on a test that is unconnected to the individual's real-life experiences. Sternberg (1985) theorized that,

> intelligent behavior is ultimately behavior that involves adaptation to, selection of, or shaping of people's real-world environments. Adaptation occurs when a person attempts to achieve a "good fit" with the environment he or she is in. Selection occurs when a person decides to find a new environment rather than adapt to the one he or she is in (such a decision might be motivated by a decision that the present environment is morally reprehensible or is unsuitable for one's talents or interests, and so on). Shaping of the environment occurs when a person cannot select an environment that seems suitable. In this case the person makes changes in the environment he or she is in, in order to improve its fit with his or her abilities, interests, values, etc., capitalize on

his or her strengths, and compensate for his or her weaknesses. (p. 18)

A Developmental View of Giftedness

The theory of intelligence and giftedness as fixed and innate human traits also came under attack from another quarter. Developmentalists had found through their own studies that the environment which nurtures (or fails to nurture) a gifted child has a profound effect on the development of his or her abilities:

> Differing from trait views, the developmental view sees each child as proceeding through several sets of stages, each stage succeeding the one before it. . . . Because the developmental framework emphasized progress within specific fields or domains of knowledge, it leads to selection criteria and program features directly related to particular kinds of excellence. (Feldman 1979, p. 662)

A psychologist specializing in child development, David Feldman proposed that neither IQ nor ancestry predict prodigiousness. Based on a longitudinal study of children who performed at or near the level of professionals at a very early age, he concluded that prodigies develop as a result of a "coincidence" (1984, p. 26). In other words, unusual ability must coincide with a nurturing environment and excellent teaching. He cites the burgeoning of talent in particular talent areas at particular times as evidence of this coincidence. For instance, the great writers and musical geniuses of the 18th and 19th centuries possessed not only musical gifts but also inhabited a cultural environment that allowed these gifts to develop.

Benjamin Bloom (1985) also propounded the developmental view, particularly emphasizing the importance of the home environment as a critical factor in the growth of a child's intellect and ability. In the early 1980s, Bloom studied the lives of 120 young adults who had performed at the highest levels of achievement possible in their fields. The subjects included musicians, sculptors, research mathematicians, research neurologists, Olympic swimmers, and world-class tennis champions. In all six of these fields, Bloom concluded that "a long and intensive process of encouragement, nurturance, education and training" was a central factor in the success of all subjects (p. 3).

While Feldman and Bloom do not minimize the importance of ability or personality characteristics, they emphasize the role of the environment as a deciding factor in the development of a child's potential into actual productivity and achievement. Supporting these contentions, educators E. Paul Torrance, Alexinia Baldwin, E.M. Bernal, and others cite the role that impoverishment and prejudice has had on the stunted growth of gifted urban students. Such students lack not only a nurturing environment but also an appropriate education to provide the academic and creative nourishment they need. Gifted students who thrive often come from families that, despite difficult living conditions, have nurtured and fostered their children's abilities and instilled a value for education.

Personality Characteristics

Although high intelligence is central to giftedness, the two are not synonymous. Terman's longitudinal studies determined that personality factors play a significant role in achievement. The four traits he identified in the highest achievers were: persistence in the accomplishment of ends, integration toward goals, self-confidence, and freedom from inferiority feelings (Terman and Oden 1947).

Other researchers have studied the personality traits of highly creative, productive adults. Roe (1952) conducted an intensive study of the characteristics of 64 eminent scientists and found that they all were highly autonomous and self-directed. Bloom's (1985) study of individuals who reached the top of their fields in six talent areas in the arts, sports, and cognitive fields led him to conclude that all 150 subjects were characterized by an unusually strong willingness to work, and all had made achievement in their talent field a top priority in their lives.

Renzulli (1978) theorized that giftedness included three essential components: ability, creativity, and task commitment. He concluded that "although no single criterion should be used to identify giftedness, persons who have achieved recognition because of their unique accomplishments and creative contributions possess a relatively well-defined set of three interlocking clusters of traits" (p. 182). Some gifted specialists who believe that the three traits provide a balanced and defendable basis for selecting students for gifted programming have adopted Renzulli's definition.

F. Gagné (1985, 1991) expanded on S. J. Cohn's (1981) model of giftedness and Renzulli's (1978, 1986) "three-ring" definition of giftedness. Gagné made a clear distinction between "gifts" and "talents." Giftedness refers more to a child's potential and ability, while talent signifies actual performance. To Gagné, giftedness means above-average *ability* in intellectual, creative, socio-emotional, sensorimotor, and other domains; and each of these includes specific strengths. Talent is above-average *performance* in particular fields of knowledge, such as mathematics or visual arts, and results from a confluence of interests, personality traits, and environment.

Morelock (1996) and Richert (1997) see giftedness and talent in hierarchical and separate ways, with the former as general intelligence and the latter as specialized aptitude. Other educators prefer the term *talent* (for example, Colangelo and Davis 1997) to *gift*. They resist the notion of a hierarchy of ability and feel that the term *gifted* tends to place academic potential above other abilities. In the course of a lifetime, what really affects an individual's achievement is not intelligence or aptitude alone but the combination of these attributes with personal traits that encourage growth.

To find out more precisely what these traits are, Walberg (1982, 1988) studied the lives of more than 200 eminent men from artistic, scientific, religious, and political fields between the 14th and 20th centuries. Versatility, concentration, perseverance, and effective communication skills occurred repeatedly among these individuals. In the field of literature, Bryant (1989) and Smith (1991) both noted common characteristics of early readers, such as high interest in learning, preference for independent work, inquisitiveness, perfectionism, good judgment, and long attention span. This research provides some useful insight into the personal qualities that accompany gifted behavior among a wide number of eminent and high-achieving individuals.

While this information may expand our understanding of giftedness, it has some limitations. As the developmentalists would point out, these personal characteristics are less likely to occur in environments that do not nurture ability. Differences in home environments (urban or rural poor, troubled family) may obscure high potential and present what appears to be an underachieving, socially insecure, or emotionally withdrawn child. Likewise, gifted students from other cultures may exhibit characteristics that differ from those identified by theorists from the dominant culture.

Other research on personality characteristics has focused on the emotional world of gifted people, which has proven to be far more complex than Terman at first proposed. When he reported on what he saw as personal characteristics common to gifted, he provided strong evidence against a stereotype prevalent during his time — the gifted as sickly, weak, and neurotic. However, in resisting this myth he inadvertently created another. Today, fortunately, a more balanced view exists, which is that giftedness includes a range of affective qualities. In 1991, the Columbus Group offered this definition of giftedness:

> Giftedness is asynchronous development in which advanced cognitive abilities and heightened intensity combine to create inner experiences and awareness that are qualitatively different from the norm. This asynchrony increases with higher intellectual capacity. The uniqueness of the gifted renders them particularly vulnerable and requires modifications in parenting, teaching and counseling in order for them to develop optimally. (Morelock 1992, p. 14)

A gifted child may at times exhibit an extreme perfectionism, a high level of sensitivity, intensity; and the child may feel out of sync with peers. Knopper (1994) observed that giftedness often includes characteristics such as curiosity, abstract thinking, frustration (with uneven development), impatience with perfectionistic expectations of themselves and others, intense interests, and a sense of humor.

A number of researchers have looked at exceptional individuals in attempting to discern the role and importance of personality. For example, Dabrowski studied the world's great moral leaders, artists, and scientists to understand their distinguishing characteristics. He evolved a developmental theory that included what he termed "overexcitabilities." Dabrowski theorized that the commonly observed intensity in gifted people results from these overexcitabilities and heightened capacity to respond to environmental stimuli (Dabrowski and Piechowski 1977). Exploring psychomotor, sensual, intellectual, imaginational, and emotional overexcitabilities, Dabrowski provided a useful language for educators to observe and understand the complex ways that gifted children experience, interpret, and respond to the world around them. Meckstroth (1998), in a review of Dabrowski's work, makes a useful analogy for understanding this: "Most of us are wired to receive five channels. Others come equipped with cable. Some have a satellite dish. They receive and respond to signals of whose existence people are not aware" (p. 296). Gifted students have this quality of fine-tuning, or hyper-awareness, which enables them to notice things others do not, think up ideas that would not occur to peers, and feel conflicting emotions based on a deeper understanding of the moral implications of a situation.

Creativity

For some researchers, creativity is the highest level of cognitive functioning (Guilford 1967; Torrance 1969). A wide range of abilities has been explored under the creativity category, but the four most widely known abilities, from Guildford and Torrance, are:

- fluency (generating many ideas)
- flexibility (creating different thought patterns)

- originality (producing unique, unexpected ideas)
- elaboration (extending ideas, embellishing, implementing ideas)

Davis and Rimm (1994) add a number of other, related abilities, such as sensitivity to problems, defining problems, visualization, evaluation, analysis, synthesis, transformation, intuition, and concentration. Wallace (1986) and Cropley (1997) see the creative process similarly and in terms of phases:

- intention (identifies problem and wants to solve it)
- preparation (applies knowledge to examine problem thoroughly)
- incubation (mulls over problem)
- illumination (sees solution to the problem)
- verification (evaluates new idea)
- communication (shares new information)
- validation (recognizes value of idea)

Many gifted people have creative abilities, but individuals whose giftedness lies primarily in the creative domain face unique challenges in conventional programs for the gifted. They can also have an unsettling effect on adults who find their thinking and learning styles too unconventional. Creatively gifted students tend to diverge from the beaten path with the solid conviction that they have discovered a new solution to a problem. These children often are very independent and occasionally stubborn and rebellious. They frequently ignore conventions and rules and may be sloppy or chaotic in executing even the simplest tasks. Sometimes they mull over straightforward questions or problems for long periods of time because they see many different ways to go about answering them.

Cultural Differences

Another group of researchers and educators who support students who diverge from the beaten path of giftedness are those who study cultural influences on gifted behavior (Passow and

Frasier 1996; Torrance 1977). E. Paul Torrance's pioneering work on "creative positives" among minority and underprivileged gifted children, for example, made entire populations of gifted students more visible to mainstream educators. Among the list of "creative positives," Torrance (1977) included the following:

- ability to improvise with commonplace materials and objects;
- articulateness in role playing, sociodrama, and story telling;
- enjoyment of and ability in visual arts, such as drawing, painting, and sculpture;
- use of expressive speech;
- enjoyment of and skills in group activities, problem solving, and so forth;
- responsiveness to the concrete;
- responsiveness to the kinesthetic;
- humor;
- originality of ideas in solving problems;
- problem-centeredness or persistence in problem solving. (p. 26)

These abilities apply to many students who lack the advantages of a white, middle-class education, and they apply to those whose gifts function in a divergent way. Creative giftedness often is the distinguishing factor in the lives of eminent pioneers, inventors, artists, and leaders.

Concluding Thoughts

While gifted education researchers and practitioners have continued to explore the many facets of giftedness, most schools still depend on the authority of the IQ test and hold to the notion of ability as an inherited, unitary quantity. Few teachers, administrators, or gifted coordinators have the time to investigate the role of a child's home environment, curriculum, gender, and learning preferences and how these other life aspects affect school performance. In this chapter of historical highlights, my aim has been to give teachers and administrators a more expansive perspective on giftedness. I also have presented the practical problems and potential loss of talent resulting from over-dependence on standardized tests and formulaic concepts of giftedness, which are at best simplistic.

Teachers should not feel the need to have a definition that includes every conceivable kind of giftedness. Such an over-broad conception would be equally counterproductive. But knowledge of the complex nature of intelligence can inform program developers and guide them to create more equitable methods of identifying gifted children.

In Chapter Two I explore specific methods of identifying gifted children and help teachers and administrators create workable definitions of giftedness appropriate to their students and their curriculum. I encourage a closer examination of conventional assessment procedures and establish guidelines for developing alternative measures of talent.

Notes

Bernal, E.M. (1981). Special problems and procedures for identifying minority gifted students. Paper presented at the Council for Exceptional Children Conference on the Exceptional Bilingual Child, New Orleans, La.

Binet, A. (1969). The education of intelligence. In E.P. Torrance and W. White (Eds.), *Issues and advances in educational psychology.* Itasca, Ill.: F.E. Peacock.

Bloom, B.S. (Ed.). (1985). *Developing talent in young people.* New York: Ballantine.

Bryant, M.S. (1989). Challenging gifted learners through children's literature. *Gifted Child Today,* 12(4), 45-48.

Cohn, S.J. (1981). What is giftedness? A multidimensional approach. In A. H. Kramer (Ed.), *Gifted children: Challenging their potential.* New York: Trillium.

Colangelo, N. and Davis, G.A. (Eds.) (1997). Introduction and overview, *Handbook of gifted education.* 2nd ed. Boston: Allyn and Bacon.

Cropley, A. (1997). Creativity: a bundle of paradoxes, *Gifted and Talented International* 12(1), 8-14.

Dabrowski, K., and Piechowski, M.M. (1977). *Theory of levels of emotional development* (Vols. I and II). Oceanside, N.Y.: Dabor Science.

Davis, G.A. and Rimm, S.B. (1994). *Education of the gifted and talented*. 3rd ed. Boston: Allyn and Bacon.

Fancher, R. (1985). *The intelligence men: Makers of the IQ controversy*. New York: W.W. Norton.

Feldman, D. (1979). Toward a nonelitist conception of giftedness, *Phi Delta Kappan* 60, 660-63.

Feldman, D. (1984). Giftedness as a developmentalist sees it. In R. Sternberg and J. Davidson (Eds.), *Conceptions of giftedness*. New York: Cambridge University Press.

Gagné, F. (1985). Giftedness and talent: reexamining a reexamination of the definitions. *Gifted Child Quarterly*, 29, 103-112.

Gagné, F. (1991). Toward a differentiated model of giftedness and talent. In N. Colangelo and G.A. Davis (Eds.), *Handbook of gifted education*. Needham Heights, Mass.: Allyn and Bacon.

Gardner, H. (1983). *Frames of mind*. New York: Basic Books.

Guilford, J.P. (1967). *The nature of human intelligence*. New York: McGraw-Hill.

Kamin, L.J. (1974). *The science and politics of IQ*. Potomac, Md.: Lawrence Erlbaum.

Knopper, D. (1994). *Parent education: Parents as partners*. Boulder, Colo.: Open Space Communications.

Marland, S. (1972). *Education of the gifted and talented*. Vol. 1. Report to the Congress of the United States by the U.S. Commissioner of Education. Washington, D.C.: U.S. Government Printing Office.

Meckstroth, E.A. (1998). Complexities of giftedness: Dabrowski's theory. In J.F. Smutny (Ed.), *The young gifted child: Potential and promise, an anthology*. Cresskill, N.J.: Hampton.

Morelock, M.J. (1992). Giftedness: the view from within. *Understanding Our Gifted*, 4(3), 1, 11-15.

Morelock, M.J. (1996). Perspectives of giftedness: On the nature of giftedness and talent: Imposing order on chaos. *Roeper Review*, 19(1), 4-12.

Passow, A.H., and Frasier, M.M. (1996). Toward improving identification of talent potential among minority and disadvantaged students. *Roeper Review*, 18(30), 198-202.

Renzulli, J.S. (1978). What makes giftedness? *Phi Delta Kappan*, 60, 180-84.

Renzulli, J.S. (1986). The three-ring conception of giftedness: A developmental model for creative productivity. In R.J. Sternberg and J.E. Davidson (Eds.), *Conceptions of giftedness.* Cambridge, Mass.: Cambridge University Press.

Richert, E.S. (1997). Excellence with equity in identification and programming. In N. Colangelo and G.A. Davis (Eds.), *Handbook of gifted education.* 2nd ed. Boston: Allyn and Bacon.

Roe, A. (1952). *The making of a scientist.* New York: Dodd, Mead.

Smith, C.B. (1991). Literature for gifted and talented. *The Reading Teacher*, 44, 608-609.

Sternberg, R. (1984). Toward a triarchic theory of human intelligence. *Behavioral and Brain Sciences,* 7, 269-87.

Sternberg, R. (1985). *Human abilities: An information processing approach.* New York: W.H. Freeman.

Terman, L., and Oden, M. (1947). *Genetic studies of genius: The gifted child grows up.* Stanford, Calif.: Stanford University Press.

Thurstone, L.L. (1938). *Primary mental abilities.* Psychometric Monograph No. 1.

Thurstone, L.L., and Thurstone, T.G. (1954). *SRA primary mental abilities technical supplement.* Chicago: Science Research Associates.

Torrance, E.P. (1969). *Creativity.* Belmont, Calif.: Dimensions.

Torrance, E.P. (1977). *Discovery and nurturance of giftedness in the culturally different.* Reston, Va.: Council for Exceptional Children.

Walberg, H.J. (1982). Child traits and environmental conditions of highly eminent adults. *Gifted Child Quarterly*, 25, 103-107.

Walberg, H.J. (1988). Creativity and talent as learning. In R.J. Sternberg (Ed.), *The nature of creativity.* New York: Cambridge University Press.

Wallace, B. (1986). Creativity: some definitions: the creative personality; the creative process; the creative classroom, *Gifted Education International,* 4(2), 68-73.

CHAPTER TWO

Identifying Gifted Children

The identification of gifted children has attracted a great deal of debate and occasioned even more research, making the topic an "ongoing dilemma" (VanTassel-Baska 2000). School districts that attempt to establish criteria for identifying gifted children face extraordinary challenges to find practical methods that are comprehensive (using multiple criteria) and fair (recognizing diverse abilities among various populations). Today's complex views of giftedness challenge the older concept of a fixed intelligence quotient (IQ), and these newer views require schools to shift from old identification methods to new, often more complicated strategies.

Identification Challenges

Definitions of giftedness must guide identification methods. Therefore, the first challenge facing any district is to define the abilities and behaviors that educators will attempt to develop and nurture. Older definitions of giftedness stress the idea of an absolute "intelligence quotient"; more recent ones focus on multiple abilities and behaviors as they relate to home and environmental influences and specific learning contexts. Districts that hold to the older definition concern themselves with a cutoff score (or set of scores) that separates "gifted" from "nongifted" students. More progressive districts consider the educational needs of a broader range of students who manifest exceptional ability in different circumstances and at different times. Educators in these districts do not identify gifted children "for all time." Rather they recognize particular abilities and talents that need development and nurturance at specific times.

Another major challenge facing school districts is individual variance among gifted students. Recent research on intelligence has illuminated the many ways that children may manifest superior abilities. Educators who work with the gifted often report as many differences *among* gifted students as between gifted students and their less advanced peers. Highly gifted students, for example, often stagnate in programs geared toward the more numerous mildly or moderately gifted. These programs often do not challenge highly gifted students sufficiently, nor are such programs' projects and resources a significant improvement over those provided to students in the regular school program.

Another issue concerns underrepresented groups. These are populations that, historically, have felt debarred from gifted programs because of improper and unfair identification practices. Dependence on IQ and achievement tests has ignored some vital differences between culturally different gifted children and mainstream students who have a cultural advantage when taking standardized tests. Similarly, gifted children who also can be characterized as learning disabled or economically disadvantaged face challenges that can hinder the expression of their abilities. Gifted girls sometimes fall into this category. The special talents of these children too often fail to gain the recognition or support they need in schools, and this failure reinforces the public perception that identifying giftedness is an elitist enterprise.

In fact, nothing could be farther from the truth. Researchers, administrators, and teachers who have committed their lives to the cause of gifted education know that gifted students are among the most neglected school populations. These educators believe that every student should have equal opportunity to grow according to his or her ability. But for gifted children this often does not happen. VanTassel-Baska (2000) suggests that the difficulties schools face in trying to establish fair and comprehensive methods of identifying gifted children will continue until educators universally alter their beliefs about the nature of giftedness:

> Our task is not to identify only the truly gifted but also to locate students who demonstrate undeveloped potential intellectually and in specific areas including academic, artistic, and leadership domains. Our task is not to select students for all time but to select them for enhanced instructional opportunities that may benefit them at a given stage of development. (p. 39)

Using this type of approach will allow schools to assess how well particular programs are serving students over time. Are the programs meeting students' needs, and can students move in and out of these programs as their needs change? It also frees schools from having to explain to unhappy parents why their child did not get into a program because this approach gives a clear rationale for the selection methods. Selecting students primarily on their scores "feels" arbitrary to many parents, especially if they know that their children have talents in curricular areas and need to be more challenged. An open approach, in which schools offer varied options to meet diverse needs and use multiple criteria to identify eligible students, will help parents discard the perception that their child is "gifted" only if he or she gets into the program. Parents will likely support a program that focuses on meeting student needs rather than merely labeling children.

Promising Identification Strategies

Identification models proceed both from federal and state definitions and from definitions that arise from research, community needs, and parent expectations. All identification models have some limitations, but schools can adapt and complement their identification strategies to create a defensible system that suits the kinds of programs they offer. As research continues to expand our understanding of giftedness and the ways it manifests itself (especially in underserved populations), schools periodically will need to establish guidelines for new selection procedures.

Underlying Principles. Six principles for establishing identification procedures emerged in the 1980s from a national panel on identification, and they still have value today (Richert 1985, pp. 68-69):

1. Advocacy. Identification should be designed in the best interests of all students.
2. Defensibility. Procedures should be based on the best available research and recommendations.
3. Equity. Procedures should guarantee that no one is overlooked. The civil rights of students should be protected. Strategies should be outlined for identifying the disadvantaged gifted.
4. Pluralism. The broadest defensible definition of giftedness should be used.
5. Comprehensiveness. As many gifted learners as possible should be identified and served.
6. Pragmatism. Whenever possible, procedures should allow for the modification and use of tools and resources on hand.

Testing. Schools use a number of intelligence tests for assessing cognitive abilities, including the Revised Stanford-Binet Test of Intelligence and the Wechsler Intelligence Scales for Children-Revised. These are individual intelligence tests commonly used by psychologists. Problems with the newest, fourth edition of the Stanford-Binet (1986) include: a lower ceiling for highly gifted than the previous Form LM and a general lowering of IQ scores to about 13.5 points below Form LM. Similar problems can be found with the Wechsler (see analysis of tests by Davis and Rimm 1994, pp. 74-80). Group intelligence tests, such as the

Cognitive Abilities Test, the SRA Primary Mental Abilities Tests, the Otis-Lennon Mental Ability Test, and others tend to be less reliable indicators of talent, especially among students who are less gifted in verbal areas and those who think more creatively. Because these tests are timed, pressure and tension also may add another dimension to the testing situation and prevent sensitive gifted children from performing well.

For gifted students of underrepresented populations, the latest version of the Raven Standard Progressive Matrices (1998) has become one of the more equitable instruments. Underrepresented populations, such as bilingual or underprivileged, have a better chance of performing well because the Raven is a non-reading test that allows students to complete tasks using either a visual or a verbal mode. The instrument minimizes the importance of past knowledge and presents tasks in a self-teaching strategy that gives all students a more level playing field. In addition, the revision includes more complex tasks for older gifted students and the highly gifted who need a test that more adequately measures higher ability levels.

Achievement tests such as the Iowa Tests of Basic Skills, the Stanford Achievement Tests, the Metropolitan Achievement Tests, and the SRA Achievement Series continue to provide the most accurate assessment of academic talent. As with other tests, however, there are several problems: the low ceiling score for exceptionally gifted students and the inequity for those with special problems, such as language difficulties, few educational resources at home, and learning problems.

Creativity tests exist to measure the abilities of nontraditional learners and creative thinkers. One of the most effective and most popular measures is the Torrance Tests of Creative Thinking (Torrance 1966). They include verbal and nonverbal (figural) subtests and are scored for fluency (amount of ideas generated), flexibility (number of different approaches or kinds of ideas), originality and, with figural tests, elaboration (number of additional embellishments to ideas).

When intelligence or achievement tests are used to identify gifted students, the students' scores usually fall in the top 3% to

5% of the population, with an IQ of 130 generally used as a cut-off point for admission to gifted programs. However, use of this criterion can vary widely in school systems across the country, with cut-off scores ranging from 120 to 140. The use of IQ and achievement tests as the major or sole means of identifying gifted students has come under criticism. Standardized tests have proven to be inadequate measures of ability among underrepresented populations, among students who are highly creative, and among students who do not test well because of a learning disability, tension or fear about testing, or low self-esteem. In addition, districts sometimes administer tests to identify areas of giftedness for which the tests were not designed (for example, the application of an academic achievement test to identify students for programs that include creative curricula).

In selecting tests, Swassing (1985) offers the following useful questions: Are the tests valid for the group to be tested? Do the tests measure achievement or intelligence? Are the tests reliable? How do the achievement tests reflect the goals of the program in which the selected students will be placed? Wise use of tests involves locating instruments most suited to the populations and programs involved and reducing the importance of tests vis-à-vis other criteria for identifying gifted children. Schools that use tests in this way stand a greater chance of establishing an equitable and valid system of identification.

Multiple Screening Sources. Barbara Clark (1988) recommends seven screening elements: 1) self-nomination or nomination from a teacher, a principal, a psychologist, a parent, or a peer; 2) teacher reports on the student's intellectual, physical, social, and emotional functioning, as well as learning style and motivation; 3) family history and student background as provided by parents, including early development and the student's out-of-school activities and interests; 4) peer identification; 5) student inventory of interests; 6) student work and achievement; and 7) a variety of tests, including group achievement and group intelligence (p. 222). Clark's approach seeks to minimize false positives (children who appear to be gifted but are not) and false negatives (children who appear to be average but are gifted).

Using multiple elements for screening gives children who may not be nominated by teachers a chance to participate in gifted programs. Swassing (1985) points out that if schools rely solely on teachers for screening, some students could easily be missed. Gifted children can exhibit characteristics that teachers find irritating. They may dominate discussions, resist rules and procedures, use humor to manipulate, lose interest in a class lesson quickly, and distract other students by acting up. In some cases, the very behavior that suggests giftedness may also jeopardize a child's chances of being selected.

The use of multiple criteria appropriate to these elements not only provides greater equity for children who may otherwise be excluded from gifted programs, but a broader range of screening sources also offers more detailed information on students. According to Feldhusen, Hoover, and Sayler (1990), the abilities of gifted students in the middle and high school become more differentiated. These researchers designed identification measures for these older students (Purdue Academic Rating Scales, or PARS) in different subject areas. They suggest combining this instrument with other sources, such as observations and parent consultations, and training teachers on the interpretation of the scales. This approach not only helps educators understand *if* a child is gifted, but *how*.

Identification of Nontraditional Gifted Students

Critics of traditional identification systems object to narrow and exclusive definitions of giftedness (see Smutny 2003). A growing number of educators in the field advise against the labeling and classifying of children into permanent categories. For example, Passow and Frazier (1996) call for a completely new system for identification, one that reflects current research and diverse concepts of giftedness. For school districts, the new system would entail: 1) expanding the definition of giftedness, 2) exploring other measures of ability and talent besides standardized tests and teacher recommendations, 3) including more culture-fair tests for gifted students (such as the Ravens), 4) balancing the importance of test scores with other talent indicators, and 5) establishing ongoing assessments of student performance to determine how well a program is meeting individual learning needs and what adjustments may be required to make it effective for more students.

Action research conducted by five universities under the National Research Center on the Gifted and Talented (NRC/GT) focused on the issues raised by the changing views of intelligence, diverse populations of gifted, and school reform (Navarro 2000). Today, more than ever before, there is a need to:

- reach a consensus on defining giftedness based upon current theories of intelligence;
- challenge identification practices, policies, and tools;
- collect data focused on student learning needs rather than solely on identification;
- present issues of equality in underrepresentation of minority populations;
- explore modes of authentic assessment over time. (p. 23)

At this time there is no way of knowing how many "invisible" gifted students exist in our schools. But the desire to find nontraditional gifted children has resulted in some changes in local and state identification policies (Gallagher and Gallagher 1994). All states encourage school districts to establish methods for identifying underrepresented students and to provide programs to meet their special needs. As described by Coleman and Gallagher (1992), these policies include:

- increasing public awareness of giftedness among special populations,
- establishing screening procedures that would identify a larger pool of potentially eligible students, and
- formalizing the use of multiple criteria in the identification of gifted students.

These policies recognize the fact that many underrepresented populations tend *not* to be informed about the special needs of gifted children, nor do these parents request that their children be screened for gifted programs. The policies also recognize the need to design a system that formalizes procedures for assessing student potential based on measures of ability and achievement that are different from the usual measures.

A wide range of alternative identification procedures can help teachers and administrators find nontraditional talent. Following are some of these procedures:

Assessment of Problem Behaviors. Sometimes gifted children show their abilities through so-called problem behaviors. Obstinacy, for example, can be a sign of frustration because of boredom or inactivity. Other problem behaviors include showing off, antisocial demeanor, impertinence, disruptiveness, refusal to follow directions, emotional immaturity, and underachievement. While these behaviors do not always signify giftedness, teachers and administrators should closely observe students who seem frustrated, restless, or rebellious. Underachieving gifted students frequently exhibit some of these behaviors.

Interviews. Asking children about themselves can result in some useful insights about their interests, ideas, and aspirations. The conversation should focus on questions about what the children do best, what they like, what they don't like to do in school, how they would change their school day if they could, and how they like to spend their free time. Gifted children, even shy ones, enjoy discussing their special passions and interests and often reveal abilities in conversation.

Portfolios. Another way to identify gifted students is to use portfolios, which are collections of the children's work in the school and home. Parents, teachers, and the children themselves contribute to the collection. Portfolios provide authentic assessment and evidence of abilities not visible through other means. They work especially well for underrepresented gifted children. Teacher portfolios of student work have been common in many districts. Parent portfolios that include a range of student work and activities also can be useful to support the process of identification for special populations.

Documentation of Strengths. Gifted program coordinators have devised various systems for documenting observable behaviors and abilities that indicate giftedness. Ideally, the process of identifying children's special strengths will combine checklists with anecdotal statements and cover an extended period of time so that a child's performance in different learning situations can be observed. Figure 1 (p. 31) is an example of a checklist to identify young gifted children.

In noting the strengths of students, teachers can focus particularly on children's use of language, level of questioning, strategies for solving problems, depth and breadth of information, creativity, absorption in tasks, interest in existential and spiritual questions, self-evaluation, tendency toward complexity or novelty, and ability to synthesize, interpret, and imagine.

Documentation of Sensibilities. Gifted children often have sensibilities that extend beyond those of average students. Parents and teachers can consider, for example: sensory (high level of response to sensory experience — the visible world, the sound, smell, and feel of things); empathic (responsiveness to the feelings of others, to the natural world, to others' expressions of pain or distress, and to a sense of justice); and intuitive (a sensitivity to others' attitudes, a sensitivity to atmosphere, body language, tone of voice, as well as a "feel" for possible solutions to a problem). Gifted children often have vivid imaginations, can remember minute details about how they felt and what they saw in a situation that occurred long ago, and express deep, sometimes complex emotions that can baffle adults. These sensibilities may become apparent in an argument in class, a debate over an issue, a visual expression in an art class, or a discussion about a story. They indicate abilities that may not be that visible in a child's work in the regular classroom, especially if this child is an underachiever.

Dynamic Assessment. In seeking learning potential among nontraditional gifted children, teachers can use "dynamic assessment" to establish ability level in specific areas. The process involves three stages:

1. Test or assign a task that measures present competency level.

Figure 1. Performance Checklist

- ☐ Has a long attention span for activities that interest him/her.
- ☐ Works independently and uses initiative.
- ☐ Loves books and reading activities.
- ☐ Is extremely curious about many things — asks Why? How? What if?
- ☐ Raises insightful questions about abstract ideas, such as love, justice, etc.
- ☐ Discusses and elaborates on ideas in complex, unusual ways.
- ☐ Is very interested in cause-effect relationships.
- ☐ Loves playing with number concepts and figuring out how to solve math problems in unique ways.
- ☐ Learns quickly and applies knowledge to new contexts with ease.
- ☐ Has vivid imagination and ability to improvise games or toys from commonplace materials; can generate other options for doing something on the spur of the moment.
- ☐ Is extremely creative — makes up elaborate stories, excuses; sees many possible answers/solutions; spends free time drawing, painting, writing, building, experimenting, inventing.
- ☐ Has spontaneous and whimsical sense of humor.
- ☐ Likes to play with words. Absorbs the speech patterns and vocabulary of different people and imitates them in stories, rhythms, or games.
- ☐ Is often singing, moving rhythmically, or using mime in self-expression.
- ☐ Is responsive to music and can improvise with easily memorized tunes, rhythms, or sounds.
- ☐ Is a leader in organizing games and resolving disputes.
- ☐ Is sensitive to the feelings of others, empathic in response to others' sorrows or troubles.
- ☐ Expresses concern about world problems, such as near extinction of animal species, political injustice, poverty, etc.
- ☐ Has a high intuitive gift and a willingness to follow "hunches" even if he/she cannot justify them at the moment they come.

Adapted from J.F. Smutny. (2001). *Stand up for your gifted child: How to make the most of kids' strengths at school and at home.* Minneapolis, Minn.: Free Spirit. Used by permission.

2. Teach for a level beyond present knowledge.
3. Retest to gauge learning.

This process works for underrepresented gifted students, especially those who do not perform well on standardized tests. It focuses more on learning ability than knowledge and provides useful information about how and what to teach individual students. Dynamic assessment also gives teachers insights into students' thinking processes, learning styles, and problem-solving abilities.

Concluding Thoughts

Changes in how we understand human intelligence have brought significant advances in the identification of gifted children. However, schools are not always willing to establish a newer and more comprehensive system of identification. For one thing, school districts receive funds based on their ability to certify to state authorities that identified students qualify for their programs. Because of this, many administrators feel forced to rely on standardized tests and teacher recommendations as the most reliable indicators of ability. Particularly in the case of tests, districts can establish cut-off scores that make accountability and reporting more straightforward. In addition, designing alternative measures of ability requires staff development and training, which schools cannot always afford.

It is unlikely that standardized testing will disappear as a method for identifying gifted students. Indeed, testing has its place and, depending on the instruments selected, can perform a vital function for certain kinds of gifted children. But to cast their nets over the "invisible" gifted — those who, because of language, nationality, learning disability, or some other personal situation, do not perform well on tests — districts need to create an alternative approach. This can be done without hiring consultants and ordering expensive tests. It requires that administrators and teachers avail themselves of the most current information on different methods for identifying giftedness and design a system that includes these other methods in a workable way.

Ideally, this effort will involve using some alternative assessment measures such as those discussed in this chapter and, further, employing a weighting system that does not rank one measure over any other. By becoming more aware of the limitations of traditional identification practices and the benefits of using a more comprehensive approach, teachers can include a wider range of talent and ensure that fewer eligible students are excluded from programs.

Notes

Clark, B. (1988). *Growing up gifted.* 3rd ed. Columbus, Ohio: Charles E. Merrill.

Coleman, M., and Gallagher, J. (1992). *State policies for identification of non-traditional gifted students.* Chapel Hill: University of North Carolina at Chapel Hill, Gifted Education Policy Studies Program.

Davis, G.A., and Rimm, S.B. (1994). *Education of the gifted and talented.* 3rd ed. Boston: Allyn and Bacon.

Feldhusen, J.F.; Hoover, S.M.; and Sayler, M.F. (1990). *Identifying and educating gifted students at the secondary level.* New York: Trillium.

Gallagher, J.J., and Gallagher, S.A. (1994). *Teaching the gifted child.* 4th ed. Boston: Allyn and Bacon.

Navarro, M. (2000). Review of *Contexts for promise: noteworthy practices and innovations in the identification of gifted students* by C. Callahan, C.A. Tomlinson, and P.M. Pizzat. *Communicator,* 31(2, spring), 23-25.

Passow, A.H., and Frasier, M.M. (1996). "Toward improving identification of talent potential among minority and disadvantaged students. *Roeper Review,* 18, 198-202.

Richert, E.S. (1985). Identification of gifted students: An update. *Roeper Review,* 8, 68-72.

Smutny, J.F. (2003). *Underserved gifted populations: Responding to their needs and abilities.* Cresskill, N.J.: Free Spirit.

Smutny, J.F.; Walker, S.Y.; and Meckstroth, E.A. (1997). *Young gifted children in the regular classroom.* Minneapolis, Minn.: Free Spirit.

Swassing, R.H. (1985). *Teaching gifted children and adolescents.* Columbus, Ohio: Charles E. Merrill.

VanTassel-Baska, J. (2000). The on-going dilemma of effective identification practices in gifted education, *Communicator,* 31(2, spring), 1, 39-41.

CHAPTER THREE

Program Options for Preprimary and Primary Students

Young gifted children, long neglected by educators, have become the focus of increasing research over the past decade (for example, Porter 1999; Barbour and Shaklee 1998; Smutny 1998; Clark 1997; Smutny, Walker, and Meckstroth 1997; Johnson and Ryser 1995). This is a positive trend, as it signals a wider recognition of the critical role that early identification plays in reaching gifted children in their most formative years of schooling.

There is a high price for postponing services for gifted students. By the time they reach grade three or four, which is when many districts begin special programming, they have spent three years in a state of boredom or frustration that can lead to problems in school (Smutny, Walker, and Meckstroth 1997). In some cases, these gifted students try to avoid school by making up excuses to stay at home. When they are in class, they doodle on their assignments or read books on the sly while the rest of the class learns material they have already mastered. In other cases, they act out their growing frustration to a point where teachers label them as behavior problems (Tolan 1996). Eventually, a portion of these children will lose interest in learning, develop poor self-esteem, and underachieve in class.

Identification Issues

One of the main hurdles that districts face in serving gifted students under age nine is finding a reliable system of identification that will work without requiring a great deal of time or expense. There are standardized tests for young children, which, if employed wisely, can be of some use in identification. But when used without a clear sense of their limitations, tests can potentially exclude even highly gifted children from the services they need and deserve.

One limitation relates to the nature of group tests (most commonly used in schools) that measure academic aptitude or achievement more than abstract reasoning ability. Tests such as the Otis-Lennon Mental Abilities Test, for example, ask for one right answer and include few items that demand higher-order and divergent thinking. Such a test presents problems for creatively gifted children who struggle with the mindset of these kinds of tests. The lack of more challenging test items also means that an artificial "ceiling" is created that limits the scores of gifted children.

Individual tests, such as the Wechsler Preschool and Primary Scale of Intelligence-Revised (WPPSI-R) and the Wechsler Intelligence Scale for Children-Third Edition (WISC-III), may yield a more accurate score, but even in these tests there still may be a low ceiling for some gifted children. The Stanford-Binet (Form L-M) works better for young children whose abilities exceed the level of some of the WISC-III subtests (which measure IQs up to 130). In addition, the Wallach and Kogan Creativity Battery and Torrance's Thinking Creatively in Action and Movement provide useful insights on creativity and thinking skills according to Feldhusen and Feldhusen (1998).

Some researchers conclude that standardized testing will always be an underestimation of giftedness in young children (for example, Gross 1999). Intellectual differences among young gifted children are vast and varied, and their abilities show themselves in many other ways than on test items. Examiners need to be aware of what tests might not tell about a child. For example, a student with exceptional verbal ability but less spatial and fine motor development may get only a moderately high score (Smutny, Walker, and Meckstroth 1997). For very young children, the testing situation can present additional problems. It may take an hour before these children reach their ceiling on an individual test, and by then they may be fatigued and distracted. In some cases, they may feel intimidated by the examiner. In order for the test to yield any useful information, young children need to be thoroughly prepared for the testing situation and comfortable with the examiner *before* they enter the examining room.

In Chapter Two I reviewed a number of alternative methods for assessing giftedness — comprehensive checklists appropriate for the population in the district, observations by teachers, parents, and community leaders, portfolios of the children's work, informal interviews, and dynamic assessment. In the case of young children, the only other method that needs serious attention is parent involvement. It is unfortunate that parents have a reputation for being biased observers. In fact, they possess a wealth of information at their fingertips and are the most accurate predictors of their children's potential (Louis and Lewis 1992). By the time their child is five or six years old, most parents can identify their children's abilities with precision and detail (Meckstroth 1991). In addition, they can share crucial information on their children's preferred learning styles and the areas where their children may need support, information that would take teachers months to acquire on their own.

Learning Needs

To create programs for preprimary and primary gifted children, educators must first consider their needs. Based on their work with these special children, Vydra and Leimbach (1998) have developed a useful set of tenets to help educators create appropriate learning experiences in the classroom. What young gifted students need, Vydra and Leimbach conclude, is to:

- use, develop, and understand their higher mental processes;
- use, develop, and understand their own creativity;
- interact with and experience other gifted children;
- have more in-depth exposure in key areas of learning;
- have work that emphasizes exploration, manipulation, and play;
- have curriculum presented in an integrated manner to help them understand the interrelatedness of multiple subject areas;
- have instruction qualitatively different than that of nongifted children;
- have instruction that is developmentally appropriate;
- have a focus on content as well as on process; and
- have direction in understanding and appreciating the diversity among individuals, in part to help them better understand themselves. (p. 464)

As these tenets suggest, programming for gifted children must be qualitatively different from the regular curriculum in order to provide adequate challenge for students' advanced and often more creative thinking processes. Part of this programming also must involve designing the learning environment. As defined by Smutny, Walker, and Meckstroth (1997), educators should create a classroom that,

- invites children to do things, with colorful posters and pictures, and a creative display of materials and sources;
- uses thematic instruction so that children can make connections among content areas;
- provides a wide range of materials and sources that include a higher complexity and challenge (such as three dimensional puzzles, computer programs, cultural artifacts, etc.);

- invites self-initiated, hands-on experimentation so that children can handle materials on their own and put them away when they are finished;
- has flexible seating arrangements so that individual students can work alone and groups of gifted children can gather to work on projects;
- arranges for lesson-related activity options for children who finish assignments early and need more challenging work to extend their learning;
- uses on-going assessment to determine student strengths and learning needs and whether the current program needs adjustment;
- maintains a portfolio of each child's work to document mastery and skill levels and to keep track of on-going observations and assessments; and
- involves parents in child's education by regular communications. (pp. 31-32)

Preprimary and kindergarten gifted children manifest uneven development (Terrasier 1985) and a wide range of differences in the physical, cognitive, social, and emotional domains. Programs need to develop ways to address the variety of learning needs and abilities found in any group of young gifted children.

The National Association for the Education of Young Children (NAEYC) has played a key role in fostering the idea of "developmentally appropriate practices" (Bredekamp 1987). This involvement has created greater recognition of the fact that a kindergarten or first-grade classroom may have students in a range of developmental ages, even though they all may be five or six years old. As long as educators understand that "developmentally appropriate" does not mean "age appropriate," they can use many of the teaching strategies recommended by NAEYC. A gifted four-year-old who has started reading should not be discouraged from doing so because it is not "developmentally appropriate."

On the positive side, the notion of developmentally appropriate practices has supported the creation of learning centers, in which students can engage in a variety of activities in various subjects. Children respond to assignments according to their interests, learning styles, abilities, knowledge, and past experiences. With guidance and direction from the teacher, they make choices about activities or projects and the materials and sources they will use (Cummings and Piirto 1998).

As in the components listed by Vydra and Leimbach, this kind of education program for young children emphasizes playing, exploring, taking risks, and creatively solving problems. Children advance at their own rate, and teachers use contracts and planning sheets to assess strengths and weaknesses and to track each student's progress. Cummings and Piirto note:

> In the developmentally appropriate classroom, the role of the teacher has changed. Formerly, the teacher was someone who told and imparted all of the knowledge. Now the teacher is one who extends, engages, questions, affirms, and challenges children as they are constructing knowledge. (p. 383)

Educating young children in a way that responds to their development, especially their cognitive growth, has inspired the "constructivist" approach to programming for gifted education. Based on theories (primarily Piaget 1977, 1980) about how children learn, the constructivist (or developmental) model focuses on how children *construct* their knowledge and understanding by interacting with the environment — exploring, testing, touching, questioning, and continually adapting to new information. In the constructivist classroom, the teacher creates environments and guides activities in order to stimulate cognitive growth in specific areas.

For young gifted children, Cohen and Jipson (1998) explore a model that combines a constructivist classroom with "mediated learning" and Gardner's multiple intelligences (1983). Vygotsky (1962) and Feuerstein (1980) theorized that to encourage cognitive growth, teachers need to become active *mediators* of the learning process. It is not sufficient to supply stimulating materials in an open environment and turn the children loose. Students need the mentoring and guidance of teachers to bring out their potential — teachers who recognize their abilities and mental ages and plan appropriate instruction. Gardner's theory of multiple intelligences further enhances this model by enabling children to engage in subjects through various talents, learning preferences, and interests. A classroom with these three influences — constructivist ideas, mediated learning, and multiple intelligences — encourages young gifted children to exercise choice, self-direction, and creative freedom, but not without guidance and mentoring by knowledgeable adults.

Program Models

In the 1980s, the Sid W. Richardson Foundation began a four-year national study of existing programming for "able learners" (Cox, Daniel, and Boston 1985). Not since Commissioner of Education Sidney Marland prepared his 1972 Report to Congress had there been any comprehensive examination of programming. The Richardson Foundation received 4,000 responses to surveys sent to 16,000 public and parochial school districts. They then sent a lengthier questionnaire to these 4,000 and received 1,572 replies. While not necessarily representative of all of the nation's school districts, this study compiled enough information from various kinds of districts to form a picture of which models prevail more than others and why.

Pull-Out Model. Seventy percent of the districts in the Richardson Survey use a pull-out model. Talented students spend most of their time in a heterogeneous classroom and are "pulled out" to attend classes for gifted students. The amount of instructional time in the pull-out program can range from as little as an hour to as much as a full day or more each week. There are both advantages and disadvantages to this model. Belcastro (1987) suggested these benefits:

> Students can spend time with their intellectual peers as well as regular classmates.

The regular teacher can work within a more narrow ability and skill range and focus on individual needs within this smaller range.

The gifted teacher can focus on independent projects and student interests, rather than basic skill instruction that the students already have mastered.

Pull-out programs also have disadvantages:

Gifted students may perceive a stigma associated with participation in the program.

Absences from the classroom may result in students missing important instruction.

Doing extra projects in the gifted classes and completing work missed in the regular class may result in these students being overburdened.

Because pull-out classes do not meet daily, students and teacher experience a lack of continuity, and activities and projects may have to be cut short.

There is little opportunity for the gifted teacher to integrate higher level thinking in pull-out classes with what the children do in the regular classroom.

The gifted teacher is often responsible for pull-out programs at every grade level in the school or may be itinerant, splitting the workday between several schools.

The pull-out model is a part-time response to a full-time condition. Gifted students still spend most of their day in an educational environment that is not geared to their needs.

Despite these drawbacks, the popularity of the pull-out model has continued in schools because it is fairly easy to implement and less costly than other models. Educators rarely employ the pull-out model for preschoolers, although some kindergartens use it. Another rationale for the model is that schools often are hard-pressed to justify a more comprehensive program for gifted children at a time when our nation's focus rests primarily on remediation and the improvement of test scores. This is especially true at the primary level because many teachers and administrators do not recognize the importance of early intervention for the gifted. In many cases the pull-out model is a diplomatic solution. It keeps concerned parents satisfied that the school is responding but does not alienate other constituents who feel that gifted education should not funnel away a large portion of the school's funding or resources.

Cluster Model. In a cluster program a group of gifted students are "clustered" together in a heterogeneous classroom. The teacher plans and implements activities for the group that focus on a particular body of knowledge or skill to be mastered, a problem to be solved, or a set of concepts or ideas to be applied to different situations. The effectiveness of clustering depends on how the teacher designs and manages the classroom. If the teacher varies instructional styles to meet the individual learning needs of the students (including the gifted), then the cluster model will integrate well into the classroom and create more flexibility in structuring lessons. Following are some advantages to the cluster model:

Students benefit from extended contact with gifted peers.

Cluster programs are not difficult to implement once the teacher has set up a workable structure and are less expensive than pull-out programs, which may involve the hiring of special staff.

Students can move in and out of a gifted cluster, and identification may be less rigid, resulting in a more inclusive program.

Cluster models also have some disadvantages:

Clustering can burden the regular classroom teacher who may already feel pushed to the limit.

Because clustering applies to a small group of students, it tends to be the first thing the teacher cancels when time is limited or other priorities require attention.

The cluster model, like the pull-out program, may consist of isolated enrichment that does not necessarily relate to the curriculum in the regular classroom.

Some kindergartens implement the cluster model for a few gifted students who have mastered skills and information that the other children have not (for example, beginning reading or writing). In these instances, teachers may cluster the more advanced students together to tackle more difficult books or to solve problems that require higher-order thinking. With a little extra planning, clustering can be a useful tool for differentiating instruction. Alternative assignments can be designed that stimulate real cognitive growth in young gifted children.

Acceleration. Schools that have no resources or services can still help gifted students if they are open to the idea of acceleration. By itself, acceleration is only a partial response to the needs of gifted children, but it is an essential one. Gifted children start their schooling already accelerated, and they need an education that accommodates the speed with which they learn (Benbow 1993). Contrary to the concerns of some educators and parents, moving a child to a higher grade or to a higher level in some subject areas does not pressure or push the child. As Feldhusen (1992) points out, early admission to kindergarten or first grade enables gifted children to satisfy their curiosity, hunger for learning, high energy, and intellectual need to explore and create. Allowing them to function at their academic level can significantly increase their motivation and self-esteem (Davis and Rimm 1994).

Another concern voiced by parents and educators is that the accelerated child will attend class with older children who may not accept him or her. This concern often is unfounded. The peers of most gifted students are not necessarily their age mates, and a large number of gifted students tend to make friends either with other gifted students or with older children. Associating with their intellectual peers and learning at a more accelerated pace often make gifted students feel more at home than in a classroom with their age mates (Gross 1992).

Special Class Model. Districts that have the financial and community support to serve gifted children on a full-time basis create special classes. Fewer than 40% of the respondents in the

Richardson study offer this option. The advantages to this alternative are obvious. Special classes meet the full-time needs of gifted primary students. Teachers have the time and resources to focus on the education of gifted students, rather than squeezing enrichment into the day when they can. Special classes also promote friendships among children and positive relationships between teachers and students. The curriculum tends to be integrated and interdisciplinary, applying thinking skills to a more complete range of subjects and disciplines.

However, full-time classes for gifted students cannot guarantee effective programming. The structure and curriculum must be thoughtfully prepared and appropriate for primary students, and teachers must be well equipped for the assignment. If not, the class, though populated exclusively by able students, may not serve their needs.

Some schools offer special classes for talented students at the preschool and kindergarten levels. In some cases, these are self-contained early childhood classrooms; in other schools there is movement between rooms and teachers. When talented preprimary students participate in a special class it is especially important to ensure that they enter a kindergarten or first-grade program that is equipped to challenge and stimulate them.

Special School Model. Few districts establish special schools as part of their gifted programming. But some schools evolve through an affiliation with colleges or universities or from a community of concerned parents and educators. Where they do exist, special schools offer a number of benefits to gifted children (Clark 1997; Belcastro 1987; Cox, Daniel, and Boston 1985). As with the special class model, special schools are a full-time response to the needs of gifted students, but with notable additions:

They offer more flexible scheduling and pacing.

They generate vastly more in terms of resources for gifted students, such as a well-equipped science lab, a strong fine arts center, etc.

They allow for sustained interaction among a number of students who are gifted in different ways.

Independent special schools have the freedom to explore alternative philosophies, structures, and methods that respond more specifically to their students and community.

Special schools that function within districts may attract criticism from some community members. Parents of children who did not get into the program may feel that their children were unfairly denied services. Because of the significant outlay of funds required, special schools can be an easy target for administrators keen to balance their budgets. In addition, some gifted students do not want to attend a special school that separates them from their friends in the regular school.

Because of their autonomy and the support they have from parents and children, independent special schools avoid some of these problems. Yet, without some kind of scholarship assistance, often only economically advantaged gifted children can attend these schools. Tuition tends to be high because these schools do not have access to the funds that public schools have.

Supplemental Programs. Supplemental programs may be sponsored by a district but also can be organized by an independent coalition of parents and teachers or by a university. Independent supplemental programs may serve children from several districts. There are advantages to district-sponsored programs: Districts can provide funding, facilities, equipment, and staff support. An independent program allows program developers to make the important decisions about identification methods and course offerings.

Effective supplemental programs are no different from school-day programs in requiring well-conceived and clearly stated objectives, an accepting atmosphere that encourages student independence, an integrated curriculum, and appropriate learning experiences. Programs can be as simple as a two-Sunday workshop on archeology organized by a handful of parents and teachers for a small group of interested primary students or as elaborate as a summer program involving hundreds of gifted children from many school districts.

Although supplemental programs may not occur on a daily basis, their value should not be underestimated. For young gifted children who have no support services, a series of elective classes every Saturday may offer the only challenge they receive all week. Supplemental programs do not occur often enough to satisfy these students on a daily basis. But they keep young gifted children intellectually and creatively alive at a time when they are most vulnerable, and they provide a supportive network for their families.

Teaching Strategies for Heterogeneous Classrooms

Creating programs for young students identified as gifted is not always feasible or affordable. There are educators who would argue that rather than focusing on identifying talented preprimary or primary students and setting up special programs to serve them, schools should focus on making all early childhood and primary classrooms nurturing environments for these children (Kitano 1982). The advantages to a classroom that differentiates and individualizes instruction are several:

Every child benefits from enrichment techniques used by the teacher.

The model avoids rigid selection guidelines that may miss some gifted children.

It can be applied in districts that lack the resources or funding to implement some of the other models.

To educate young gifted students in the regular classroom may involve some challenges. First, teachers who know little about gifted children need professional development and ongoing support in order to meet the needs of this population on their own. A number of teachers may find the prospect of educating gifted children overwhelming. A great deal depends on their instructional style. Teachers who already differentiate the curriculum, have flexible seating arrangements, use group work, and use alternative methods for imparting curriculum content will have little trouble helping gifted students.

Teaching to Learning Styles. By observing how children interact with new ideas and materials, teachers can identify their strengths and learning styles and plan instruction accordingly. For example, auditory learners tend to do well in traditional classrooms because the method of instruction is auditory — lecture, instructions given aloud, reading aloud, and so on. Auditory learners often think analytically. Visual learners are more holistic, preferring to grasp the "big picture" rather than analyze the pieces that constitute it. Visual learners benefit from visual aids, such as pictures, graphs, and charts; and they may enjoy creating some visual representation of new information they synthesize. Tactile-kinesthetic learners also are holistic learners, but they prefer hands-on activities that give them opportunities to test, apply, or experiment with new knowledge. To accommodate these differences, preprimary and primary classrooms often use learning centers, in which teachers guide children to sources and materials the students can use for assigned projects or activities.

Compacting the Curriculum. Compacting enables teachers to compress the basic curriculum so that gifted children can move at *their* pace, usually using less time repeating old information and more time acquiring new content and advancing their cognitive and creative gifts. This strategy involves evaluating the student to determine areas of mastery (by pretesting or requesting the child to demonstrate knowledge using an appropriate medium), evaluating content to see whether more advanced work in the subject or some other project of the child's interest might be suitable, and planning alternative experiences (sometimes with the child). At first, teachers may find the extra management and supervision burdensome. But usually, once teachers have designed a structure for establishing goals, making agreements with the child (perhaps in the form of a learning contract) and keeping records of the child's progress, then the strategy becomes almost routine. Winebrenner (1992) offers useful suggestions on how to create learning contracts that specify materials to be used, activities or projects to be pursued, and criteria for completing assigned work. She demonstrates how teachers can move gifted students in and out of whole-class instruction depending on areas of mastery and learning needs.

Parallel Curriculum. Primary teachers can apply some of the principles of this approach. The parallel curriculum model (see Tomlinson et al. 2002) offers four parallel approaches to curriculum development to ensure a rich curriculum for all learners, including the gifted. These four approaches include the core curriculum (a foundation for all others), a curriculum of connections (an extension of the core curriculum that explores connections across disciplines), a curriculum of practice (an extension focused on applications within disciplines), and a curriculum of identity (an extension focused on students' goals, interests, and abilities). This model enables teachers to create a cohesive, well-focused approach to teaching young gifted students.

Teaching Creatively. One of the benefits of creative teaching is that young students of all ability levels can advance at their own pace and level of complexity. E. Paul Torrance (1977) has proven the fundamental importance of creativity to student leaning among all age groups. For young children, it is second nature to explore, manipulate objects, question, experiment, improvise, test, and adapt. Considerable research has focused on creative behaviors, such as fluency, flexibility, originality, elaboration, problem defining, analysis, synthesis, evaluation, analogical thinking, and transformation (Torrance 1979; Bloom 1974; Guilford 1968; Gowan, Demos, and Torrance 1967). One result of this research is that more educators are now considering its application to young children and how they learn (for example, Flack 1997; Smutny, Walker and Meckstroth 1997; Stanish 1988).

For young children, creative activities can be easily worked into almost any unit. Teachers of young children have used various strategies, such as brainstorming, creative problem-solving, experimenting with different points of view, exploring ideas through different media or subjects, creative dramatics or movement, and imaginative exercises (for example, having the children pretend to be a different person, an animal, or an object).

Chapter Five contains a more exhaustive treatment of the research on creativity and creative teaching models that can be used in the regular classroom.

Using Tiered Groups. The term *tiered groups* may include cluster grouping for gifted students, but it also refers to a larger strategy for grouping in a mixed-ability classroom. Through tiered groups, teachers create activities based on the students' level of mastery, which determines what each group will do. For example, in a lesson on money a teacher may group children according to their level of abstract thinking. One group may practice counting money; another may explore the value of different coins; a third group may pretend to manage a store and explore what the items cost and how to make change. Unlike cooperative groups, in which everyone performs the same tasks regardless of ability, tiered groups tackle assignments at each group's collective pace and level of understanding. The system is flexible. Students may be in an advanced group for math but not English. Children also can move from group to group as they acquire skills and demonstrate mastery.

Forming Interest Groups. Gifted students work best with other gifted students. However, they also work well with other children who share their enthusiasm and interest in particular subjects. A highly motivated young child who may not perform at the same level as some gifted students in some areas still can make valuable contributions to a group project and may accomplish what he or she could not do before. Underachieving gifted children with interests in certain subjects often benefit from group work in which peers support and share their passions. Interest groups also are flexible. They often change from lesson to lesson, depending on the subject and the kind of learning planned by the teacher.

Using Independent Projects. For young gifted students who have been doing projects in their homes since they were able to crawl, independent work must be a part of their education. Most gifted children have strong interests, and they should not have to wait until school is over to pursue them. Independent projects fulfill several needs in young gifted children, including the need to work alone, to focus on a subject in depth, and to apply new skills and knowledge to a long-term project that interests them.

Using learning contracts, such as those suggested by Winebrenner (1992) and Smutny, Walker, and Meckstroth (1997), educators can draw up some basic guidelines on short-term goals, appropriate activities, and resources for the children to use. Once the projects have begun, teachers meet regularly with these students (and their parents, if appropriate) to monitor progress. Creating a workable system for recording and monitoring independent projects will relieve teachers of the extra work that this alternative can entail.

Involving Parents. Parents should always be considered as aids in the education of gifted young children. Many school districts have successfully used parent volunteers to assist small groups of children who need help with reading or mathematics. Rarely do schools think of parents for small groups of gifted students. Yet the parent population includes a wide range of talent and expertise. It would not be difficult to find out more about the talent and expertise in the parent community and match parent mentors with gifted children.

Concluding Thoughts

Young gifted children are among the most underserved of gifted populations. Because of the difficulties in identifying them, many states do not offer special services to gifted children until the end of grade two or three. The early school years are among the most difficult for gifted children. For the first time, they experience restraints to their progress and discover that it may be wrong to be different or to move more quickly than other children. Young gifted students from geographically remote or impoverished communities may feel "different" at home and at school. As one talented woman said, "When all the other kids in my community were learning how to ride their ponies and enter in the local 4-H shows, I was learning how to read. By age five I was begging my mother to let me borrow books from the library; I lived for those books."

Teachers and administrators who recognize the importance of early intervention can do much for these special children. They can broaden the range of criteria to include ability domains beyond what might appear in tests or in conventional pencil-and-paper assignments. If funds are not available for a comprehensive program, schools still can help this population by making the regular classroom more responsive to the needs of young gifted students. With professional development and support, teachers can design alternative learning experiences within the existing curriculum. This response will stop the youngest of our gifted children from shutting down before they have a chance to learn at a pace and level appropriate for them.

Notes

Barbour, N.E., and Shaklee, B.D. (1998). Gifted education meets Reggio Emilia: Visions for curriculum in gifted education for young children, *Gifted Child Quarterly* 42(4): 228-237.

Belcastro, F. (1987). Elementary pull-out program for the intellectually gifted — boon or bane? *Roeper Review* 9(4): 208-212.

Benbow, C.P. (1993). Meeting the needs of gifted students through use of acceleration. In M.C. Wang, M. Reynolds, and H. Walberg (Eds.), *Handbook of special education: Research and practice*, Vol. 4. Elmsford, N.Y.: Pergamon.

Bloom, B.S. (Ed.) (1974). *Taxonomy of educational objectives.* New York: McKay.

Bredekamp, S. (1987). *Developmentally appropriate practices in early childhood education: Serving children from birth through age eight.* Washington, D.C.: National Association for the Education of Young Children.

Clark, B. (1997). *Growing up gifted.* 5th ed. Upper Saddle River, N.J.: Merrill.

Cohen, L.M., and Jipson, J.A. (1998). Conceptual models: their role in early education for the gifted and talented child. In J.F. Smutny (Ed.), *The young gifted child: Potential and promise, an anthology* (pp. 390-419). Cresskill, N.J.: Hampton.

Cox, J.; Daniel, N.; and Boston, B. (1985). *Educating able learners.* Austin, Tex.: University of Texas Press.

Cummings, C., and Piirto, J. (1998). The education of talented young children in the context of school reform. In J.F. Smutny (Ed.), *The young gifted child: Potential and promise, an anthology* (pp. 380-89). Cresskill, N.J.: Hampton.

Davis, G.A., and Rimm, S.B. (1994). *Education of the gifted and talented.* 3rd ed. Boston: Allyn and Bacon.

Feldhusen, J.F., and Feldhusen, H.J. (1998). Identification and nurturing of precocious children in early childhood. In J.F. Smutny (Ed.), *The young gifted child: Potential and promise, an anthology* (pp. 62-72). Cresskill, N.J.: Hampton.

Feldhusen, J.F. (1992). Talent identification and development in education. *Gifted Child Quarterly,* 36: 123.

Feuerstein, R. (1980). *Instrumental enrichment.* Glenview, Ill.: Scott, Foresman.

Flack, J. (1997). *From the land of enchantment: Creative teaching with fairy tales.* Englewood, Colo.: Teacher Ideas.

Gardner, H. (1983). *Frames of mind.* New York: Basic Books.

Gowan, J.C.; Demos, G.D.; and Torrance, E.P. (Eds.). (1967). *Creativity: Its educational implications.* New York: John Wiley.

Gross, M.U.M. (1992). The use of radical acceleration in cases of extreme intellectual precocity. *Gifted Child Quarterly,* 36: 91-99.

Gross, M. (1999). Small poppies: Highly gifted children in the early years. *Roeper Review* 21(3): 207-14.

Guilford, J.P. (1968). *Intelligence, creativity and their educational implications.* San Diego: Robert R. Knapp.

Johnson, S.K., and Ryser, G. (1995). Identification of young gifted children from lower income families. *Gifted and Talented International* 9(2): 62-68.

Kitano, M. (1982). Young gifted children: Strategies for preschool teachers. *Young Children* (May): 212-13.

Louis, B., and Lewis, M. (1992). Parental beliefs about giftedness in young children and their relation to actual ability level. *Gifted Child Quarterly* 36(1): 27-31.

Meckstroth, E.A. (1991). Guiding the parents of gifted children. In R.M. Milgram (Ed.), *Counseling gifted and talented children: A guide for teachers, counselors, and parents* (pp. 95-120). Norwood, N.J.: Ablex.

Piaget, J. (1977). *The development of thought: Equilibration of cognitive structures.* New York: Viking.

Piaget, J. (1980). *Adaptation and intelligence: Organic selection and phenocopy.* Chicago: University of Chicago Press.

Porter, L. (1999). *Gifted young children: A guide for teachers and parents.* St. Leonards, NSW, Australia: Allen and Unwin.

Smutny, J.F.; Walker, S.Y.; and Meckstroth, E.A. (1997). *Teaching young gifted children in the regular classroom.* Minneapolis, Minn.: Free Spirit.

Smutny, J.F. (Ed.) (1998). *The young gifted child: Potential and promise, an anthology.* Cresskill, N.J.: Hampton.

Stanish, B. (1988). *Lessons from the hearthstone traveler: An instructional guide to the creative thinking process.* Carthage, Ill.: Good Apple.

Terrasier, J.C. (1985). Dyssynchrony: Uneven development. In J. Freeman (Ed.), *The psychology of gifted children* (pp. 265-74). Chicester, England: Wiley.

Tolan, S.S. (1996). *Is it a cheetah?* www.stephanietolan.com (not available in print).

Tomlinson, C.A., et al. (2002). *The parallel curriculum: A design to develop high potential and challenge high ability learners.* Thousand Oaks, Calif.: Corwin.

Torrance, E.P. (1977). *Creativity in the classroom.* Washington, D.C.: National Educational Association.

Torrance, E.P. (1979). *The search for satori and creativity.* Buffalo, N.Y.: Creative Education Foundation.

Vydra, J., and Leimbach, J. (1998). Planning curriculum for young gifted children. In J.F. Smutny (Ed.), *The young gifted child: Potential and promise, an anthology* (pp. 462-75). Cresskill, N.J.: Hampton.

Vygotsky, L.S. (1962). *Thought and language* (E. Hanfmann and G. Vakar, trans.). Cambridge, Mass.: MIT Press.

Winebrenner, S. (1992). *Teaching gifted kids in the regular classroom.* Minneapolis, Minn.: Free Spirit.

CHAPTER FOUR

Program Options for Elementary and Secondary Students

What kinds of program are appropriate for gifted students at the elementary and secondary levels? Educators and researchers have responded to this question with a variety of philosophies and views about how best to serve the learning needs of America's most able students. Most of their responses fall into one of several broad categories. However, these categories should not be seen as mutually exclusive, because many programs include some or all of the approaches discussed in this chapter. The categories should be viewed as distinctions in emphasis, rather than differences in content.

The broad categories are three: acceleration, enrichment, and differentiation. The first response focuses on gifted students' need for an *accelerated* program of instruction that allows them to move rapidly through fundamental skills and knowledge to more challenging aspects of a subject or field of study. This strategy is thought to be especially important in school subjects that are learned sequentially, such as mathematics. Implicit in this response is the definition of gifted children as students who learn more rapidly than their peers.

The second general response emphasizes the need for *enriched* curricula, which explore topics in greater depth and breadth. Literature, science, and social studies are subjects that lend themselves to the development of enriched curricula. Students with special aptitude in these areas benefit from learning situations in which they can tackle complex and abstract ideas. The implicit definition of gifted students in this context focuses on their preference for complexity, flexible thinking, and wide range of learning styles.

The third general response examines the need for *differentiated,* or *individualized,* curricula that allow independent study projects built on self-selected topics or individual interests. Curricula developed to meet the individual needs of gifted students are open-ended. Students pursue their own interests and develop research abilities or specific creative gifts, with the support and mentoring of program personnel. An independent study or differentiated curriculum may involve acceleration and enrichment and enables students to function as researchers or creators in a self-selected talent area. The implicit definition of giftedness in this context is that exceptional abilities and potential manifest themselves in individual ways that should be supported in school, even if the children's interests are outside the regular curriculum.

These three responses represent three general categories of curriculum models for gifted education. All three have had a significant influence on gifted program development and generated a number of useful models for elementary and secondary schools. They have also caused some controversy among researchers and specialists as to which approach most effectively serves the learning needs of the gifted. Such controversy has encouraged more educational alternatives for gifted students.

Those who support acceleration tend not to do so at the expense of enrichment (Stanley and Benbow 1986; Stanley 1978).

Rather, they argue that enrichment fails to challenge or enhance the abilities of gifted children *unless* acceleration underlies it. Those who focus on enrichment (for example, Schiever and Maker 1991) do not exclude acceleration. In fact, it could be argued that an enriched curriculum for gifted students would naturally involve students acquiring skills and information more quickly than in the regular curriculum.

As for differentiated curricula, students often experience the benefits of both accelerated and enriched content as they work independently in a chosen subject. However, more needs to be done to develop individualized or differentiated curricula for gifted children and young people. Scholars working with target populations — such as highly gifted (Gross 1993), creatively gifted (Piirto 1992), culturally different (Frasier and Passow 1994; Torrance 1977), urban poor (Borland and Wright 1994), and others — have made the field more sensitive to the differences between groups of gifted students as well as between individuals.

To provide an overview of the trends in gifted programming, this chapter includes examples of well-known curricula and program models available in each of these three broad categories. Most include all of the categories to some extent.

Acceleration

The various forms of acceleration involve moving the gifted child ahead of his or her age or grade mates. Sometimes this movement is into a higher grade. Other forms of acceleration involve course content more than physical advancement.

Grade Advancement. One way to accelerate the curriculum for the gifted child is to move the child into a higher grade than his or her age mates. For example, a gifted fourth-grader might move into sixth grade instead of fifth upon completing the fourth-grade year. Early college admission is a similar option at the high school level.

Parents and educators need to consider a student's social maturity and academic readiness before deciding on grade advancement. Many districts, in fact, do not permit students to skip grades as a matter of policy (Davis and Rimm 1994). Schools often voice concerns about the skills and knowledge the accelerated child may miss, as well as social difficulties in the higher grade. However, research has shown that mature gifted students, when given appropriate support during the transition, adjust well and benefit from a more advanced curriculum (Rimm and Lovance 1992; Southern and Jones 1992; Van Tassel-Baska 1986).

If this option becomes a possibility, educators need to assess skill gaps and allow a trial period to see how the child responds to the new environment (Feldhusen 1992). Parents of gifted children also need to understand that most school systems do not permit early admission to junior or senior high school (Davis and Rimm 1994). Ideally, a gifted student should skip a grade before entering junior or senior high. Early college entrance also can be an unpopular option with school districts. In cases where a student demonstrates social maturity and an intellectual readiness for college-level work, however, parents, teachers, and school counselors may be able to convince the district to make an exception.

Advanced Studies. A number of variations are possible that allow students to engage in advanced studies, often for college credit, during high school. Some schools and colleges permit students to earn high school credits and college credits simultaneously. Others offer students the opportunity to begin college considerably advanced in terms of required classes.

One of the variations is the Advanced Placement (AP) program, sponsored by the College Board. It provides college-level courses and exams for high-ability students in many areas, including English literature and composition, foreign languages, science and mathematics, history, and others. The exams are yearly and include a 90-minute multiple-choice and 90-minute essay test. Colleges differ in their policies regarding AP credit. Some do not accept any credit; others accept credit but differ in how much AP credit can be applied to a college program.

The International Baccalaureate (IB) program is another variation, which provides an opportunity to earn college credit. IB programs, often found in private schools, are highly selective and include foreign language and international studies (Cox and Daniel 1991).

Colleges and universities also have taken a role in developing advanced study opportunities. The Math Talent Search, which resulted from the Study of Mathematically Talented Youth (SMPY), is widely recognized and emulated. Developed at Johns Hopkins University by Julian Stanley, the program is designed to provide "mathematically precocious" students with a radically accelerated mathematics curriculum. Stanley's research demonstrated that mathematically precocious students can master the content of courses that have been compressed and accelerated (Stanley, Keating, and Fox 1974). Another study on developing verbal talent offers similar guidance on appropriate teaching strategies for gifted students in specific content areas (Van Tassel-Baska, Johnson, and Boyce 1996).

Compacted Curricula. Curriculum compacting permits gifted students to move through a body of knowledge at a quicker pace. Compacting works best in subjects that are studied sequentially, such as mathematics. The following steps are typically involved in compacting:

> The teacher establishes criteria for demonstrating mastery, sometimes in consultation with parents, a counselor, or a gifted program coordinator.
> The teacher identifies content to be eliminated.
> The teacher adds advanced content to a child's program, usually in consultation with the student, parents, and the gifted program coordinator.

This process operates in a cycle. As the student completes the new content added to the program, he or she demonstrates mastery through a test, written examples, an experiment, or some other measure. Then the student continues to accelerate through the curriculum, meeting alternative goals and assignments. Using an organizing form — such as *The Compactor* (Renzulli and Smith 1978) or Winebrenner's sample (1992, p. 14) — will allow the teacher, parents, and other school personnel to negotiate the details of a gifted student's program and determine criteria that will ensure satisfactory progress.

Enrichment

Enrichment without higher-order thinking processes provides little challenge for gifted students. Davis and Rimm (1994) offer a comprehensive list of curriculum objectives within the following categories:

Maximum achievement in basic skills, based on needs, not age;

Content and resources beyond the prescribed curriculum;

Exposure to a variety of fields of study;

Student-selected content, including in-depth studies;

High content complexity — theories, generalizations, applications;

Creative thinking and problem solving;

Higher-level thinking skills, critical thinking, library and research skills;

Affective development, including self-understanding and ethical development; and

Development of academic motivation, self-direction, and high career aspirations. (p. 123)

These categories integrate acceleration, enrichment, and individualized instruction. They balance the breadth and depth of study that enrichment offers with an accelerated and individualized curriculum. Students conduct in-depth research and use higher-order thinking, but they also acquire skills and knowledge at an accelerated pace. Without the challenge of advanced subject matter and the demand for analytical thinking, enrichment programs simply cannot provide the education gifted students need (Stanley and Benbow 1986).

Pull-Out Programs. Pull-out programs remove selected students from the regular classroom once or twice a week to meet with the gifted resource teacher. Students and teachers agree on a topic, such as architecture, electricity, ecology, or fantasy writing, and design a series of activities related to the topic. Gifted program coordinators often choose a model for developing curriculum and planning activities. For example, Feldhusen's Three-Stage Enrichment Model develops creative thinking and problem-solving and focuses on research and independent learning (Feldhusen and Kolloff 1986). In a three-stage process children gradually develop increasingly sophisticated abilities to solve problems and learn how to design and execute their own research projects.

While students generally enjoy pull-out programs, there is little research to demonstrate such programs' long-term effects. The degree to which this enrichment involves advanced thinking and accelerated learning (rather than just a series of stimulating activities any child could do or enjoy) determines the success or failure of the program.

Supplemental Programs. Gifted programs outside of schools vary in their objectives and course offerings. While some tend to focus more on accelerated instruction in subjects like math and science, others expose gifted students to subjects not taught in the regular schools and emphasize application, invention, and creative problem-solving. Offered on weekends and during the summer months, these programs play a pivotal role in helping gifted children discover and define their interests, explore new concepts, and take creative risks. (See Chapter Eleven for more information on this option.)

Mentorships. Mentoring can provide acceleration, enrichment, and individualized instruction for gifted children with specific interests (Kerr 1991; Torrance 1984). In most cases, mentorships occur outside the school, and parents make the arrangements. There may be cases, however, when a science teacher, for example, mentors a gifted child who wants to research a particular phenomenon or to prove a hypothesis. In either case mentorships require assessment of learning needs, setting goals, and periodically reviewing the mentoring relationship to ensure that the child is progressing and that the program meets his or her needs.

Mentorships also should be considered for gifted high school students who need career awareness and exposure to a variety of fields of study.

Governors' School Programs. The Governors' School Program concept began in the early 1990s and has grown steadily. A state-supported summer residential school for gifted teenagers, such programs offer classes in math, science and technology, the arts and entertainment, and the humanities and social studies. Governors' School Programs are another type of opportunity for gifted students to explore subjects in greater depth than they could in the regular classroom.

Specialty Camps. Camps may not be designed exclusively for gifted students, but specialty camps routinely provide advanced instruction in specific areas, such as music (Interlochen comes to mind), art, computers, foreign languages, and so forth. Most students who attend these camps have talents in these areas and come highly motivated to learn. Gifted students enjoy the long hours of dedicated effort in acquiring new information and benefit from associating with other young people who are equally focused and interested.

Published Enrichment Packages. Another form of enrichment involves using published programs, such as the Junior Great Books Program. The Junior Great Books Foundation trains teachers to lead in-depth discussions and to ask questions that require interpretation and analysis. Teachers can adjust the program to match the ability levels of their students. Students not only sharpen their reading and listening skills but also analyze psychological and social realities, philosophical issues, and literary styles to present their own hypotheses and conclusions.

A number of other national programs and projects can be adopted as part of a gifted curriculum. Odyssey of the Mind (Micklus 1986) is an excellent example. Featured in science magazines and newspapers, this program aims to increase the creative problem-solving ability of children by challenging them with complex problems to solve in original ways. Working as a team, students brainstorm possible solutions to a problem, select their best solution, and create the machinery or process needed to put their idea into action. Their ideas are then compared and tested in competitions with teams from other schools. The curriculum for this program models itself on the hands-on problem-solving curricula of the physics departments of some of the best engineering schools in the country. The competitive structure gives the program a sports-like dimension.

A similarly structured national program is the Future Problem Solving Bowl developed by E. Paul Torrance. In this competitive program, students develop creative problem-solving skills. After training, teams of students work together on complex real-life problems. Within a time limit, the students research the problem, generate solutions, test and select their best solution, and write a report to enter into a regional competition. The curriculum goals of this project emphasize research and communication skills as well as strategies for solving problems creatively. (Further information can be obtained from Future Problem Solving Program, 2028 Regency Road, Lexington, KY 40503-2309. Phone: (800) 256-1499. Fax: (859) 276-4306. E-mail: FPSolve@aol.com. Online at www.fpsp.org.)

Academic Decathlon is another packaged program. It is designed for high school students and includes regional, state, and national competitions. Each school competes in one of the following: conversation skills, essay writing, formal speech, economics, language and literature, fine arts, mathematics, physical science, and social studies. It also features a Super Quiz. (Further information can be obtained from United States Academic Decathalon, P.O. Box 1868, Los Alamitos, CA 90720-1868. Phone: (562) 626-0092. Fax: (562) 626-0098. E-mail: info@usad.org. Online at www.usad.org.)

Differentiated Curriculum

A number of approaches to differentiating curriculum and instruction can effectively meet the individual learning needs of gifted students.

Renzulli's Enrichment Triad. Joseph Renzulli (1977) created the Enrichment Triad Model as a significantly differentiated and therefore defensible gifted program model. While Renzulli's model could be seen as an enrichment model, its primary goal is the development of an *individual's* ability to research, investigate, and solve real problems. The mechanism for achieving this goal is a curriculum model with three distinct parts, or "types" of enrichment:

Type 1 enrichment consists of activities that awaken interests, provoke inquisitiveness, and stimulate children to pursue a new talent or interest area. Field trips, interest centers, visiting resource persons, games, films, and other introductory learning experiences help students identify interest areas for further study.

Type 2 enrichment provides training in systems, processes, and skills that enable the students to find information, conduct investigations, and solve problems in any interest area of their choice. Brainstorming, scientific method, and values clarification are examples of the types of processes that engage students in an Enrichment Triad program.

Type 3 enrichment is the ultimate goal of the program. At this stage, the teacher assists the student in selecting a specific interest area and identifying a gap in knowledge or a problem to solve. The student then investigates the topic, forms and tests ideas, and creates original solutions or products. Student products serve as the means of communicating findings and are evaluated by program personnel with the goal of helping the student to revise and improve his product.

Renzulli's Enrichment Triad program is held in high esteem by gifted program personnel but often is modified in one way or another because of the time, energy, and resources it requires to work well. Each of the three types of enrichment requires the use of significantly different teaching strategies and styles. Renzulli himself encourages teachers to modify and adapt this model to suit the particular needs and resources available to them.

Schoolwide Enrichment Model. An adaptation of Renzulli's earlier Revolving Door Model (Renzulli, Reis, and Smith 1981), the Schoolwide Enrichment Model (Renzulli and Reis 1985) is one of the most popular programming models today. Based on the Enrichment Triad Model, SEM serves a significantly larger portion of a school's students, perhaps 15% to 20%. Renzulli's "talent pool" concept enables schools to avoid charges of elitism and to relax stringent criteria that often exclude students in the target populations and others who do not perform well on standardized tests. Individual students can develop skills, explore interests, and find intellectual and artistic challenge in the projects they conceive and pursue.

The "schoolwide" nature of the model appeals to educators. Renzulli and Reis provide detailed information on how to incorporate Type 1 and 2 enrichment (appropriate for all students) into the regular curriculum. Many students benefit from Type 2 activities that focus on identifying interests and developing the skills needed to implement potential projects. For Type 3 enrichment, students need to request permission to pursue their project on a form called a "Light Bulb — an Action Information Message." This enables highly motivated students not included in the "talent pool" to attempt a project idea that interests them.

Students in the talent pool benefit both from Type 3 enrichment (which is highly individualized and also effective for highly gifted students) and from the model's curriculum compacting option. Renzulli and Reis's comprehensive book on schoolwide enrichment guides educators through each step of this model and provides useful forms for every imaginable need.

Self-Directed Learning. Treffinger (1986) developed a curriculum model called Self-Directed Learning. This model increases the independent learning skills of each child. Treffinger recognizes that even children with unusual capacities for learning may not be able to work independently unless they are provided with experiences and training in independent management. He describes a four-step plan for encouraging self-direction and a curriculum model that enables children to progress from levels 1 to 4. The model begins with activities, timeline, end products, and evaluation criteria largely determined by the teacher. By level

4, however, the student assumes responsibility for these components. The products of all four levels are evaluated by the student and the teacher, but the child assumes greater responsibility for self-evaluation as he or she reaches level 4.

Individualized Educational Plans (IEPs). A number of school districts have adapted the special education model of Individualized Educational Plans to their gifted programs. In this structure, the curriculum is decided by gifted specialists, psychologists, and other personnel to fit the specific strengths and deficiencies of each identified student. A curriculum plan will specify activities, resources, and expectations for the student's particular talents, problems, learning styles, and interests. For example, a gifted bilingual child with special abilities in science and math may undertake advanced research, experiments, and projects while also receiving support for her communication skills in English.

Differentiation Within Classrooms. Differentiated classrooms design learning options with individual abilities, interests, and learning profiles in mind. By differentiating instruction, a heterogeneous classroom can meet the needs of gifted students by modifying content (subjects to be learned and materials needed), process (activities used), and products (vehicles for showing and extending what has been learned). These modifications occur through strategies already discussed in this and previous chapters.

With cutbacks in funding for gifted education, differentiation within classrooms has drawn greater interest from school districts. Researchers, such as Carol Tomlinson (1999) and Diane Heacox (2002), have created teacher-friendly guides for responding to individual learning needs. The principles are fairly consistent. To modify *content*, a teacher may use curriculum compacting, enrichment activities, learning contracts, or cluster grouping. A teacher who uses a thematic, broad-based, and integrative curriculum can more easily differentiate content for gifted students than one who does not. To modify *process*, the teacher designs more complex projects or activities that demand higher-level thinking (creative as well as academic) in order to challenge gifted students. Instead of practicing skills or absorbing factual information, the student draws on logic, analysis, and creative thinking to solve problems, explore issues, create stories or poems, or design a science experiment. To modify *products*, a teacher creates a range of media for students to demonstrate what they have learned. Ideally, this enables students to represent their knowledge and ideas through their preferred learning styles. One student may write biographical fiction based on research, while another student might conduct an experiment with the class to demonstrate a major finding of his or her study.

Parallel Curriculum. As outlined in Chapter Three, the parallel curriculum (Tomlinson et al. 2002) allows regular classroom teachers to work with any of four approaches: core curriculum, curriculum of connections, curriculum of practice, and curriculum of identity. So doing can increase the challenge, complexity, and interest for all students. While still too new to be fully tested, this model promises a comprehensive system for teachers who want all of their students to benefit from a richer curriculum. It demands that teachers rethink the aims of the curriculum and devise methods for students to build on knowledge, skills, and concepts along a continuum of ascending intellectual demand. It draws on many of the principles of differentiation and focuses them through the four parallel strands.

Casting a Wider Net

For almost three decades educators have experimented with gifted program models and structures. Most have found that no one model meets the needs of the widely diverse student populations they serve. One of the most comprehensive plans for integrating various methods, approaches, and models into a districtwide program has been proposed by June Cox in *Educating Able Learners* (Cox, Daniel, and Boston 1985). The final chapters of this book outline "a comprehensive approach to programming that will bring together all the resources of a community to meet as wide a range of abilities as the resources will allow" (p. 121). The approach is illustrated by imagining an ideal district with the commitment and resources devoted to discovering and nurturing talent by "casting a wide net" to include all children who might benefit from gifted programming.

Called the Pyramid Project, Cox's approach offers both acceleration and enrichment and allows for and encourages individual differences. One of the cornerstones of the Pyramid Project is a district commitment to appropriate pacing or continuous progress in academic subjects such as reading and math. As individual students demonstrate mastery in these subjects, they progress to more advanced work:

> Whether the districts accelerate the educational process by moving bright students to higher grade levels in their areas of accomplishment or by bringing advanced materials down to the students, this provision is expected to meet the needs of many able learners in the regular classroom. (p. 158)

The broad base of the pyramid represents the enrichment needed by a large number of able learners. Various enrichment activities can be provided for all students in the regular classroom, for example, the Type 1 enrichment activities described by Renzulli. Additional enrichment would target highly motivated students with special abilities and interests. Gifted behavior units can inspire these students to pursue their own ideas through research and experimentation. Interscholastic competitions, such as science fairs, Future Problem Solving Bowl, and Odyssey of the Mind, can stimulate and challenge those who want to explore a topic in depth.

The middle tier of the pyramid is designed to provide unusually advanced learning opportunities for those students who require them. Cox suggests the use of honors classes and dual enrollment for students who need radical acceleration in certain subjects. Highly gifted elementary students may be placed in middle or high schools for certain subjects, such as math. A few exceptional high school students may enroll in college-level courses.

The top tier of the pyramid is reserved for students whose needs cannot be adequately met in their existing school or district. These students may require placement in academies and special schools devoted to gifted education of one type or another. States such as North Carolina and Illinois have established special residential high schools for students with extremely high aptitudes in math and science. In many cities, magnet high schools are devoted to talent areas, such as the performing arts, math and science, or the International Baccalaureate (IB). The IB is a special high school curriculum that was developed in Geneva, Switzerland, in 1970. As already mentioned, the IB curriculum requires mastery of two languages and includes special courses in history and the social sciences with a multicultural perspective.

Concluding Thoughts

Most districts are not "ideal" in the way Cox has outlined and do not command the resources to develop such a comprehensive system. However, every district can integrate approaches and models that include various kinds of gifted students and that reach a variety of learning needs. Based on an ongoing assessment of the student population, schools can combine acceleration, enrichment, and differentiated instruction to develop students' abilities in effective and appropriate ways. Highly artistic students could develop their creative gifts while also accelerating through material they have already learned on their own. Highly able science students could explore more advanced subjects in science with the goal of designing their own experiments or investigating a new line of research.

This kind of programming demands a new emphasis in gifted education. The energy and resources for programming focus more on curriculum development and the delivery of services to students, rather than on sorting students into in-groups and out-groups. Whole-school programs involve the whole school community in their efforts. Classroom teachers deliver certain elements of the program while specialists support, coordinate, and teach specialized segments of the program.

There is no single way to create or maintain such a program. Each program, each district, requires an interactive assessment of needs and gaps in the existing school program, a search for meaningful alternatives to fill these gaps, strong communication of goals and objectives, and constant vigilance for ways to improve every element of the program. In this way, more gifted children will be appropriately served.

Notes

Borland, J.H., and Wright, L. (1994). Identifying young, potentially gifted, economically disadvantaged students. *Gifted Child Quarterly* 38(4): 164-171.

Cox, J. and Daniel, N. (1991). The International Baccalaureate. In R.E. Clasen (Ed.), *Educating able learners* (pp. 157-66). Madison, Wis.: Madison Education Extension Programs, University of Wisconsin-Madison.

Cox, J., Daniel, N., and Boston, B. (1985). *Educating able learners.* Austin: University of Texas Press.

Davis, G.A., and Rimm, S.B. (1994). *Education of the gifted and talented.* Third Edition. Boston: Allyn and Bacon.

Feldhusen, J.F. (1992). Talent identification and development in education. *Gifted Child Quarterly* (36): 123.

Feldhusen, J.F. and Kolloff, P.B. (1986). The Purdue three-stage enrichment model for gifted education at the elementary level. In J.S. Renzulli (Ed.), *Systems and models for developing programs for the gifted and talented* (pp. 126-52). Mansfield Center, Conn.: Creative Learning Press.

Frasier, M.M., and Passow, A.H. (1994). *Toward a new paradigm for identifying talent potential.* Storrs, Conn.: National Research Council for the Gifted and Talented.

Gross, M.U.M. (1993). *Exceptionally gifted children.* New York: Routledge.

Heacox, D. (2002). *Differentiating instruction in the regular classroom: How to reach and teach all learners, grades 3-12.* Minneapolis, Minn.: Free Spirit.

Kerr, B. (1991). *A handbook for counseling the gifted and talented.* Alexandria, Va.: American Association for Counseling and Development.

Micklus, S. (1986). *Odyssey of the mind program handbook.* Glassboro, N.J.: OM Association.

Piirto, J. (1992). *Understanding those who create.* Dayton: Ohio Psychology Press.

Renzulli, J. (1977). *The enrichment triad model: A guide for developing defensible programs for the gifted.* Wethersfield, Conn.: Creative Learning.

Renzulli, J.S., and Reis, S.M. (1985). *The schoolwide enrichment model: A comprehensive plan for educational excellence.* Mansfield Center, Conn.: Creative Learning.

Renzulli, J.S.; Reis, S.M.; and Smith, L.H. (1981). *The revolving door identification model.* Mansfield, Conn.: Creative Learning.

Renzulli, J., and Smith, L. (1978). *The compactor.* Mansfield Center, Conn.: Creative Learning Press.

Rimm, S.B., and Lovance, K.J. (1992). The use of subject and grade skipping for the prevention and reversal of underachievement. *Gifted Child Quarterly* (36): 100-105.

Schiever, S.W., and Maker, C.J. (1991). Enrichment and acceleration: An overview and new directions. In N. Colangelo and G.A. Davis (Eds.), *Handbook of gifted education* (pp. 99-110). Needham Heights, Mass.: Allyn and Bacon.

Southern, W.T., and Jones, E.D. (1992). The real problem with academic acceleration of gifted students. *Gifted Child Quarterly* (33): 29-35.

Stanley, J.C. (1978). Identifying and nurturing the intellectually gifted. In R.E. Clasen and B. Robinson (Eds.), *Simple gifts.* Madison, Wis.: University of Wisconsin-Extension.

Stanley, J.C.; Keating, D.P.; and Fox, L.H. (Eds.). (1974). *Mathematical talent: Discovery, description and development.* Baltimore: Johns Hopkins University Press.

Stanley, J.C., and Benbow, C.P. (1986). Youths who reason exceptionally well mathematically. In R.J. Sternberg and J.E. Davidson (Eds.), *Conceptions of giftedness* (pp. 361-87). New York: Cambridge University Press.

Tomlinson, C.A. (1999). *The differentiated classroom: Responding to the needs of all learners.* Alexandria, Va.: Association for Supervision and Curriculum Development.

Tomlinson, C.A., et al. (2002). *The parallel curriculum: A design to develop high potential and challenge high ability learners.* Thousand Oaks, Calif.: Corwin.

Torrance, E.P. (1977). *Discovery and nurturance of giftedness in the culturally different.* Reston, Va.: The Council for Exceptional Children.

Torrance, E.P. (1984). *Mentor relationships: How they aid creative achievement, endure, change, and die.* Buffalo, N.Y.: Bearly.

Treffinger, D.J. (1986). Fostering effective, independent learning through individualized programming. In J.S. Renzulli (Ed.), *Systems and models for developing programs for the gifted and talented.* Mansfield Center, Conn.: Creative Learning.

Van Tassel-Baska, J. (1986). Acceleration. In C.J. Maker (Ed.), *Critical issues in gifted education* (179-196). Rockville, Md.: Aspen.

Van Tassel-Baska, J.; Johnson, D.T.; and Boyce, L.N. (Eds.). (1996). *Developing verbal talent: Ideas and strategies for teachers of elementary and middle school students.* Boston: Allyn and Bacon.

Winebrenner, S. (1992). *Teaching gifted kids in the regular classroom.* Minneapolis, Minn.: Free Spirit.

CHAPTER FIVE

Understanding and Serving Creatively Gifted Students

Many scholars and educators have researched creativity over the past few decades. In this chapter I highlight the most influential scholarship on creativity and explore teaching models and activities that can meet the needs of children with creative and artistic gifts. There are three major sections to the chapter. The first explores the nature of creativity, notably in two subsections: a way of being (feelings, attitudes, characteristics) and a way of thinking and doing (cognitive processes, problem-solving behaviors, artistic expression). The second examines strategies that schools have used to develop creative ability. The third explores ways of integrating the arts into the regular curriculum.

The Nature of Creativity

It is not uncommon to think of creativity manifested in two ways: a way of being and a way of thinking and doing.

A Way of Being. Creative expression is a vast phenomenon, extending beyond narrow, conventional contexts to life itself. We can refer to the creative attitude or the creative experience, for example, without looking for tangible proof of either. Maslow (1968) saw creativity as a way of being, which he called "self-actualization." Self-actualized human beings live lives of spontaneity and freedom. Unhampered by concerns over others' opinions, they give themselves license to be original.

Self-actualized human beings distinguish themselves not by membership in an artistic elite but by their keen "sense of wonder" (Carson 1965). Puzzling paradoxes intrigue rather than frighten them. They prefer to seek the unknown than to settle into familiar answers because of some nagging need for security. Their "peak experiences" (Maslow 1968) or "encounters" (May 1975) imply a creative way of being distinct from either talent or training.

May (1975), Maslow (1968), Carson (1965), and Rogers (1954) noticed several primary characteristics of imaginative people:

- Total immersion in the moment (experiencing a temporary suspension of time, past and present);
- Openness to experience as an original event (leaving the past behind and treating the present as new); and
- Complete self-acceptance (judging one's self independently of others and validating one's own individuality without reservation).

In this sense, creativity is a state of mind more than a product. Highly creative children focus all of their energy on discovery and invention, which is why so many struggle when forced to restrict themselves to the limits — the end points — of knowledge. Charles Kettering once commented that an inventor is "a fellow who doesn't take his education too seriously" (in Guilford 1968, pp. 84-85). Creative people do not let what they know define how they should act in a given situation.

In addition to the classic four Guilford/Torrance abilities described in Chapter One (fluency, flexibility, originality, elaboration) and other characteristics explored in detail by Torrance (for example, 1962, 1980, 1984), Davis and Rimm (1994) also observed such traits as independence, energy, enthusiasm, adventurousness, curiosity, humor, intuitiveness, a love for the complex and mysterious, and a need to work alone. Sternberg (1988) noted that creative learners tend to be tolerant of ambiguity, especially in problem-solving situations. Creativity is not simply a gift or ability but underlies the very nature of some children. It determines how life is experienced, how problems are perceived, how duties are performed, how instruments are played, and how visions are realized.

Understandably, creative students struggle in any setting where there is only one way to process information or to do an assignment. Authority-oriented adults may misconstrue the creativity of some students and consider them rebellious or stubborn. Often creative children wonder what is wrong with them that they cannot just do what everyone else is doing. The difference they feel lies not simply in the way they behave but in the way they receive and experience the world. Because this is not something they can change, many frustrated creative children remain unaware of their gifts and critical of their failure to meet the standards of the school.

Whitehead observed: "Fools act on imagination without knowledge; pedants act on knowledge without imagination" (in Parnes 1967, p. 7). Because of the pressure to deliver a certain amount of content to students and to help them score well on standardized tests, teachers have a completely different mindset from the creative student in their classroom. Creative thinkers relate to knowledge as an ongoing process and are generally more interested in questions than answers. While knowledge consumers collect and compile data, inventors question those files, analyze information, probe weak links, and explore and apply innovative ideas. For this reason, creative people often agitate those who wish to keep things as they are. By investigating gaps in knowledge and questioning old assumptions or theories, they break down the old system, which makes room for something new to emerge.

A Way of Thinking and Doing. There is a part of the creative process that remains an enigma. How do artists, inventors, and writers discover their ideas? What guides their unconventional meanderings, sudden leaps of faith, and risky experiments? Where do the lines of critical and creative thinking intersect? Researchers can describe a series of stages that take place when a new discovery occurs or the changes in perception that lead to a flash of insight, but they cannot account for the means by which a creative person suddenly finds a novel approach to a problem. The eminent French mathematician Poincaré noticed that behaviors leading up to discovery typically involve a period of labor, a period of rest, and an illumination, followed by additional labor (to solidify illumination).

Poincaré's famous story (1913) about how he discovered Fuchsian groups followed this pattern. After many days of working on a solution to his problem, he let the matter rest, drank a cup of black coffee, and then discovered what he termed "Fuchsian functions." Later, Poincaré was stepping into a bus when another idea occurred to him with no conscious effort at all. He realized that the transformations he "had used to define the Fuchsian functions were identical with those of non-Euclidian geometry" (p. 37). He later verified this discovery, which made a significant advance in mathematics.

What actually happened in that moment? We can trace the process that led up to it, but conscious thought did not originate Poincaré's discovery. Arieti (1976) suggests: "Certainly it is plausible to view the creative process as going through the stages of preparation, incubation, inspiration, and verification, but it is also so for the solution of any problem" (p. 18). The illumination stage in creative thinking is the only one that actually creates. On the other hand, conscious thought prepares for this "magic moment." It stretches everything known to the limit and then waits. From there, the process eludes researchers.

The Wallas Model. The stages described by Wallas (1925) — preparation, incubation, illumination, and verification — conform to Poincaré's description of the creative process. In the preparation stage, a person defines a problem and explores relevant information and sources. Incubation involves letting the problem and information "simmer" for a while; it may also entail free-writing in a notebook and experimentation or improvisation. During illumination, as Poincaré describes, a solution or new idea suddenly appears. In the final verification stage, the creative person works out the details of the discovery or invention, thus demonstrating its workability.

Creative Problem Solving Model (CPS). Osborn (1963) founded this model of five steps — fact finding, problem finding, idea finding, solution finding, and acceptance finding. Updated by Parnes (1981) as well as Treffinger and his associates (for example, Treffinger and Firestien 1989), this model emphasizes both divergent thinking (generating many ideas) and convergent thinking (choosing the most promising or inspired possibilities). It takes a systematic approach to a mysterious process and gives individuals specific directions for each step. In *The Magic of Your Mind* (1981), Parnes takes readers through a wide range of sample problems to illustrate how the model works in various contexts. Briefly, the steps in the CPS Model involve the following activities:

Fact finding. List all known facts about problem. (Parnes recommends who, what, when, where, why, and how questions.)

Problem finding. Consider various ways of perceiving and defining problem. (How problem is defined determines its solution.)

Idea finding. Generate ideas through divergent thinking and brainstorming.

Solution finding. Establish criteria for evaluating idea. (What are the conditions for satisfaction?)

Acceptance finding. Consider audiences who would accept the plan and explore steps to make the idea responsive to their concerns.

Perhaps the most significant step in this process is problem finding. Einstein observed, "The mere formulation of a problem is far more often essential than its solution, which may be merely a matter of mathematical or experimental skill" (in Parnes 1967, p. 129). Getzels and Csikszentmihalyi (1972) in their study of artists' behavior cited the formulation of problems as a good predictor of creativity in finished products. The problem-solving process indicative of imaginative thinkers may be revealed in the following six questions:

- Has the problem been formulated before by the problem solver?
- By anyone else?
- Is a correct method of solution known to the problem solver?
- To anyone else?
- Is a correct solution known to the problem solver?
- To anyone else?

When students invent their own problems rather than respond to the ones handed to them, they have an opportunity to discover and originate novel ideas.

Artistic Expression. Creative individuals often express themselves through the arts — music, dance, mime, theater, and visual art. These media enable gifted students to draw on other "intelligences" (Gardner 1983) to tap their creative potential. Kinetic, auditory, and visual learners who may not show their creativity in one of the problem-solving models may perform more freely through musical, theatrical, or artistic activity.

Artistic giftedness is a powerful source for creative work. Seeley (1989) argues that the arts enhance sensitivity, self-expression, and creative responses to complex problems. Goertz (2001, 1990) observes that artists sharpen observation, abstract thinking, and problem analysis. "The artist visualizes and sets goals to find and define the problem, chooses techniques to collect data, and then evaluates and revises the problem solution with imagination in order to create" (2001, p. 476). Students with theatrical gifts examine and improvise with situations and problems from multiple points of view, often considering "what if" scenarios. Music students can express their sensitivity to sound and rhythm in creative writing (both poetry and prose); they can perceive patterns, sequences, and use logic that illuminates problems in novel ways.

In the regular classroom, creatively gifted children may not distinguish themselves as high achievers nor test well at the end of the school year. They show their potential in a wide range of behaviors. For example, they:

- Generate many ideas on how to tackle a problem in group work;
- Ask questions, such as, "Can I do it this way instead?";
- Enjoy experiments or any activity where a solution to a problem is unclear;
- Excel in visual art, theater, dance, music, or language arts (see Torrance 1979 and 1981 on creative ability in kinesthetic or auditory areas);
- Demonstrate originality of thought and expression in writing and class discussions;
- Are quick to explore alternative approaches to a baffling problem rather than repeat the steps of a known formula or solution;
- Have a quick wit and enjoy playing with words and expressing humorous insights;
- Seem driven by a curiosity about many things and ask probing questions;
- Can visualize or imagine the combination of elements or ideas before testing them;
- Demonstrate exceptional mental agility in adapting laws, processes, or ideas from one context and applying them to another;
- Are comfortable with ambiguity and what others might consider a chaotic work space; and
- Have an intuitive sense about what might work without knowing precisely why.

This is by no means a comprehensive list, but it shows where teachers need to look for creative behaviors in the regular classroom.

Strategies for Developing Creative and Artistic Ability

Developed by individuals in a range of professions, the strategies that follow have proven to be effective means for enabling students to solve challenging problems through creative and imaginative thinking. While some students certainly possess more creative ability than others, all benefit from processes that encourage discovery, invention, and original thought.

Brainstorming. The name most associated with brainstorming techniques is Alex Osborn (1963). He was a strong proponent of what he called "deferred judgment," in which students postpone any evaluation of an idea until later. The goal of brainstorming is to produce many ideas or solutions in a relaxed and open-ended learning environment. Premature evaluation can interfere with this process and possibly abort an inspired idea.

Osborn created four ground rules for brainstorming:

Criticism is ruled out (judgment should not interfere with process);

Free-wheeling is welcomed (wild ideas can become innovative solutions);

Quantity is wanted (a long list of possible ideas is the goal); and

Combination and improvement are sought (ideas in modified or more elaborate form create more options).

Following this process, a teacher can guide the class in evaluating the ideas presented. Because evaluation always is part of the creative process, students need to experience this step in a guided format. Creative children can be severe critics and may lack the skills needed to assess their own work in a productive way. By including evaluation in a brainstorming session, teachers can instruct students on the most effective method for critiquing their ideas. Points to consider in a group evaluation session might include:

Consider aspects of a problem that are different from ideas listed;

Examine the values applied to an idea and whether or not they are valid (for example, a judgment of "ridiculous" to a seemingly far-out idea may be more a reflection of the criteria used than the idea itself);

Avoid judgments that are personally directed at the creator of an idea; and

Explore different ideas in a flexible and imaginative way.

Attribute Listing. This strategy by Crawford (1978) assumes that any step taken in a creative process depends on changing an attribute of something or applying that same attribute to something else. There are two forms of attribute listing: attribute modifying and attribute transferring. In attribute modifying, students list main attributes of something (for example, in the case of a bicycle these may include size, color, speed capacity, style of locomotion, and seating arrangements) and then come up with ideas under each main attribute. Bicycles designed for two people would be an example of attribute modifying.

In attribute transferring, students engage in analogical thinking: They apply attributes from one situation or object to another. To use the same example, a student might design a bicycle with directional signals similar to those used for cars. Another student might imagine how the handlebars could be redesigned to include a radio or cassette player with built-in speakers.

Idea Checklists. Checklists can be useful in helping students generate ideas about how to improve on or transform an object, idea, or solution. Osborn's *73 idea-spurring questions* (1963) have proven effective as catalysts for creative thinking. His questions encourage students to think about different uses of an idea, specific attributes that parallel other ideas (and thereby suggest new uses), and different combinations, rearrangements, and changes that could lead to new, creative ideas. The checklist strategy for teaching creative thinking has been termed the SCAMPER method: Substitute, Combine, Adopt, Modify-Magnify-Minify, Put to other uses, Eliminate, Reverse-Rearrange (Stanish 1988).

Synectics Methods. Creative people often combine elements that, on the surface, do not appear related. Gordon (1961) established guidelines for what he considered an unconscious process of creative thinkers to draw analogies between disparate elements. Evolved from his work with creative groups, Gordon originally designed these strategies for adults and then later adapted them for children (1974). He focused on four types of analogies: direct, personal, fantasy, and symbolic.

In direct analogy, students might consider how the natural world solves problems that also face human beings, such as the need for shelter. Architectural structures have direct connections to nature. Exoskeletons became the model for a whole range of enclosures, from domes to ordinary homes, while vertebrates provided another model for much higher buildings, skyscrapers. Without the idea of designing a "spine" for tall buildings, skyscrapers would not endure as they have.

In personal analogy, students imagine how it would feel to be in the position of a particular object. The charming children's book, *Corduroy,* is an example of this. More than just an imaginary exercise, personal analogies can generate interesting perspectives. Particularly helpful in creative writing, personal analogy can present challenges such as these:

> As Colin Powell's jacket, write an essay about a trip when he wore you for an important international event or meeting.
>
> You are Emily Dickinson's pen. Choose a poem and describe the writing of this poem from your point of view.
>
> Write a mystery in which you, as a vacuum cleaner in a hotel room, inhale something under the bed that solves a crime. How will you let the police know that you have solved the crime?
>
> Compose a poem from the point of view of yourself as a tree. It can be about what you see in your neighborhood or how you like the season's changes or how a local resident saved you from being chopped down.

In fantasy analogy, creative thinkers present solutions that seem unrealistic and fanciful. Students address questions such as:

How can my room clean itself? What would make it possible for everyone to enjoy doing their taxes? As far out as these questions seem, they stretch imagination in ways that can sometimes lead to solutions. Self-cleaning ovens, for example, must have begun with this kind of thinking. Children who lean toward inventing often use fantasy analogy without knowing it.

In symbolic analogy, students analyze two-word phrases that seem contradictory. Examples include: serious humor, gentle anger, youthful senility, openly secretive. The problem created by this conflict between words can stimulate thinking in new directions. Students can explore situations and contexts in which humor makes people laugh and cry at the same time or where the seriousness of the message conflicts with the comical way a writer or performer presents it. Ideas can evolve from symbolic analogy. For example, someone exploring the concept of "gentle anger" might create a program that helps people to use their anger in diplomatic ways.

Synectics helps teachers to insert creative moments into the regular curriculum or can add a new dimension to creative problem-solving activities. It also can stretch the imagination in cases where students feel "stuck" or at a loss for any new ideas to try. Students can "restart" with questions: How is a tree like a star? How is solving this math problem like reading a mystery? How is a book like a whale? Creative children enjoy this kind of mind-bending exercise, and such an exercise can lead to a new thought. Discoverers and inventors have happened on their solutions by making these kinds of combinations. The previous example of Poincaré points this out, where he suddenly realized that the transformations he used for Fuchsian functions were the same as those of non-Euclidian geometry.

Integrating the Arts into the Curriculum

Creative children always benefit from integrating the arts into the regular curriculum. As demonstrated by Smutny, Walker, and Meckstroth (1997), teachers can use the arts as a catalyst for extending higher-level thinking in language arts, social studies, math, and science. When integrated with the curriculum, the arts stimulate divergent thinking, apply the imagination to problem-solving and reasoning, and generate more alternatives for creativity and self-expression. Following are a few examples:

> In a historical study, children create an imaginary life (sketch, draw maps, write biographies, dramatize scenes, paint portraits of imagined happenings).
>
> In a study of culture, children examine traditions and cultural institutions (listen to music of the region, view art, perform dances, tell and write stories).
>
> In a language arts class, children write in response to art and music (compose free verse poems from paintings and pictures, create stories based on musical scores).
>
> In a study of ecology, children research an animal species for creative production (create animal narratives, write poems, sketch cartoons, paint animal environments).
>
> In a mathematics class, children explore geometric concepts (explore relationships between cubism and geometry, make connections between musical scores and mathematical ideas, invent math problems through story-telling, represent math concepts through paintings and sketches).

Integrating the arts into the curriculum can benefit students of all ability levels. For creatively gifted students, the use of visual and performing arts stimulates new ways of perceiving, sensing, analyzing, and solving problems. Following are examples of poetry activities that draw on the arts. I have used these activities focused on exploring poetic language in classes for gifted students through the Center for Gifted at National-Louis University.

- *Writing free verse.* Poetry presents an extraordinary challenge that is at once artistic, creative, analytical, and intuitive. Gifted students can explore the power of metaphoric language, the poetic quality of words, and the complexity and subtlety of meaning by writing free verse. Without the constrictions of a rhyme scheme, they are free to focus on imagery and point of view and to experiment with different writing styles.

- *Creating a group poem.* The teacher may begin by writing a free verse poem with the students before they work on their own. For example, the teacher might begin by showing a painting or a picture. The students think about the "atmosphere" of the image — the color, the feelings they get from it, and what certain images might mean. Some students may struggle to find the right words to portray what they feel. They may need to consider questions such as: If you were to think of the people (or animals) in this picture as colors, what colors would they be? If you were to think of them as music or sound, what would you hear? If they had texture or temperature (such as cold, smooth, warm, liquid, etc.) what might they be? After a questioning period, the teacher begins to ask for lines to create the poem. Individual students contribute them, each building on the previous sentence or phrase, each suggesting some new aspect of the world they are observing. As the students offer their ideas, the teacher writes them on the board so that everyone can read and build on them. Once the students have shared, the teacher reads the poem and then the class discusses the images created and what they convey.

- *Presenting catalysts.* The students are now ready to work on their individual poems. The teacher provides a wide range of creative catalysts (for example, paintings, pictures, films, musical recordings) and guides students in deciding what they will use. Sources for writing poetry are indispensable, whether they present a general theme or provide a variety of possible topics. Again, focused questions and directions stimulate original thinking. For example:

  Notice the picture of Jane Goodall in this photo. What is she staring at? What exists outside the lines of the painting? What does her expression tell you? What do you imagine has just happened before this picture was taken?

Pick an animal or person in this short film. Write down what you feel, see, hear, taste, and sense around you. Write short phrases, images to create the world of this film according to your chosen subject.

Look at the architecture of this nineteenth century New York neighborhood. Imagine living there yourself. What sounds do you think you'd hear on this street? Walk down this street and imagine what you would see, who would you talk to, and what you might smell as you passed the shops.

The point is to make the catalysts accessible to the students in creative ways — to encourage them to enter other worlds and then create vivid images of their perceptions and imaginary experiences. Unburdened by the obligation to stick to a rhyme scheme, many gifted writers produce some extraordinary verse. The example below was written by a fifth-grade student.

A mournful sky
    Shivering
Casting waves of unhappiness through her veins
    Thoughtful limbs
Reach upward to plant a kiss on a frowning thought
    comforting
    A seed
Soon to change the color of Mother sky to a rich healthy sapphire blue
    that will burn away her black cape of troubles
    Melt them down to tiny drops
    Letting them fall away to cool the Earth
    Then thank her fellow trees
And invite them up her stairway for tea, as an honor for their kindness

— Kendall, grade 5

Another vehicle that students can use to connect the arts with literature is chamber theater. Chamber theater offers extraordinary benefits to creative, kinesthetic learners — a largely underserved population — and stimulates both imagination and higher-order thinking. Gifted students particularly enjoy analyzing and interpreting text, exploring motivation, selecting important episodes, and contributing their ideas to the staging process. While the teacher may make final decisions about which scenes in a story or historical account to include in a chamber theater production, students should participate in their selection in some way. Following are the two main steps for using chamber theater.

- *Divide the text.* Students break into small groups and each one works with a portion of a text. The text might be a passage of historical nonfiction or a piece of fiction. They then answer questions, with one student noting down the answers: What is this section about? Who are the important characters? What problems do they face and how do they solve them? What are the most exciting scenes and why? What is most important in this text as it relates to the whole story? Afterward, each group shares their thoughts about their portion of the text and why they think certain scenes should be included in their theatrical adaptation. The teacher uses their ideas and comments when making the final selection of scenes to be dramatized.
- *Stage the play.* It is important for everyone to have a some role to play in the chamber theater production — as actor, narrator, set designer, artist, sound technician, or script writer. The teacher must find out which students in each group have particular talents in areas such as set design and sound, so that they can form teams to work on this aspect of the play when the class begins to rehearse. To ensure maximum participation, the students should not have to memorize lines, especially if the production is for the rest of the class or another class.

Individuals and groups make important decisions in each of these two primary activities. For example, each group decides collectively how to stage the scene or scenes they have chosen. What should the narrator say, and what lines are for the actors? How can the production convey certain episodes? Should the narrator say the lines while the actors mime the scene? Could some of the story be conveyed through song or dance? Who has those talents? What is the best use of sound effects?

The teacher can decide how far to take the activity. Time constraints may limit the number of scenes, for example. Will there be time, talent, and funds for other elements, such as music, sound effects, props, or costumes? In adapting a written text for the stage, students grapple with problems of interpretation. The teacher will need to facilitate debates and discussions and may need to step in occasionally and make decisions in order to keep the process moving forward.

Some gifted students need to act and construct in order to learn most effectively. Assuming another identity can enable students to make a story their own, to explore points of view and the tension created by conflicting viewpoints. In the selection and staging of scenes, gifted children exercise higher-level thinking as they explore the demands that one art form (theater) impose on another (literature) and the changes and adjustments they need to make to transform a text into a theatrical event. The act of creating a physical reality out of a written narrative is a stimulating process that helps students appreciate the dramatic power of narrative in a completely new way.

Concluding Thoughts

Students with creative and artistic abilities struggle in classrooms where the dominant way to learn is to receive, record, and reproduce information. To some extent, all gifted children are creative. But some students think so divergently that they may not appear gifted at all. Most of them feel, at one time or another, that their creative being is somehow wrong, inconvenient, irritating to others, and something to suppress in order to get along in school. At the same time, their creative gifts constantly urge them to try the unbeaten path, to synthesize information in original ways, to invent alternative solutions, and to imagine worlds beyond "the known."

A fourth-grader once said, "Most of the time, I just try to figure out what the teacher wants and do it. After school, I can be myself again." Creative students should not have to wait until after school to be themselves. A great many models exist that can guide these students to do creative work in the context of almost any subject. Integrating the arts into the curriculum also gives them the freedom to use their unique talents and learning styles to think, perceive, reason, compare, synthesize, and discover. Gifted students crave this freedom to create. Providing them with tools that enhance creative thinking and opportunities to use creative media will prepare our most imaginative and innovative minds for a lifetime of contribution.

Notes

Arieti, S. (1976). *Creativity: The magic synthesis.* New York: Basic Books.

Carson, R. (1965). *The sense of wonder.* New York: Harper and Row.

Crawford, R.P. (1978). The techniques of creative thinking. In G.A. Davis and J.A. Scott (Eds.), *Training creative thinking.* Huntington, N.Y.: Krieger.

Davis, G.A., and Rimm, S.B. (1994). *Education of the gifted and talented.* 3rd ed. Boston: Allyn and Bacon.

Gardner, H. (1983). *Frames of mind.* New York: Basic Books.

Getzels, J.W., and Csikszentmihalyi, M. (1972). Concern for discovery in the creative process. In A. Rothenberg and C.R. Hausman (Eds.), *The creativity question.* Durham, N.C.: Duke University Press.

Goertz, J. (1990). The role of art in cognition: A problem solving approach. In S. Bailey, E. Braggett, and M. Robinson (Eds.), *The challenge of excellence: "A vision splendid."* New South Wales, Australia: Australian Association for GT in Association with the World Council for GT Children.

Goertz, J. (2001). Searching for talent through the visual arts. In J.F. Smutny (Ed.), *Underserved gifted populations.* Cresskill, N.J.: Hampton.

Gordon, W.J.J. (1961). *Synectics.* New York: Harper and Row.

Gordon, W.J.J. (1974). *Making it strange.* Books 1-4. New York: Harper and Row.

Guilford, J.P. (1968). *Intelligence, creativity and their educational implications.* San Diego: Robert R. Knapp.

Maslow, A.H. (1968). *Toward a psychology of being.* 2nd ed. New York: D. Van Nostrand.

May, R. (1975). *The courage to create.* New York: W.W. Norton.

Osborn, A.F. (1963). *Applied imagination.* 3rd ed. New York: Scribner's.

Parnes, S.J. (1967). *Creative behavior guidebook.* New York: Scribner's.

Parnes, S.J. (1981). *The magic of your mind.* Buffalo, N.Y.: Creative Education Foundation.

Pioncaré, H. (1913). Mathematical creation. In B. Ghiselin (Ed.), *The creative process: A symposium.* Berkeley: University of California Press.

Rogers, C. (1954). Towards a theory of creativity. In P.E. Vernon (Ed.), *Creativity: Selected readings.* Suffolk, England: Richard Clay, Ltd.

Seeley, K. (1989). Arts curriculum for the gifted. In J. VanTassel-Baska et al. (Eds.), *Comprehensive curriculum for gifted learners* (pp. 300-13). Boston: Allyn and Bacon.

Smutny, J.F.; Walker, S.Y.; and Meckstroth, E.A. (1997). *Teaching young gifted children in the regular classroom.* Minneapolis, Minn.: Free Spirit.

Stanish, B. (1988). *Lessons from the hearthstone traveler: An instructional guide to the creative thinking process.* Carthage, Ill.: Good Apple.

Sternberg, R.J. (1988). Three-facet model of creativity. In R.J. Sternberg (Ed.), *The nature of creativity* (pp. 125-47). New York: Cambridge University Press.

Torrance, E.P. (1962). *Guiding creative talent.* Englewood Cliffs, N.J.: Prentice-Hall.

Torrance, E.P. (1979). *The search for satori and creativity.* Buffalo, N.Y.: Creative Education Foundation.

Torrance, E.P. (1980). Assessing the further reaches of creative potential. *Journal of Creative Behavior,* 14, 1-19.

Torrance, E.P. (1981). Non-test ways of identifying the creatively gifted. In J.C. Gowan, J. Khatena, and E.P. Torrance (Eds.),

Creativity: Its educational implications. 2nd ed. Dubuque, Iowa: Kendall/Hunt.

Torrance, E.P. (1984). Teaching gifted and creative learners. In M. Wittrock (Ed.), *Handbook of research on teaching.* 3rd ed. Chicago: Rand-McNally.

Treffinger, D.J., and Firestien, R.L. (1989). Update: Guidelines for effective facilitation of creative problem solving. *Gifted Child Today* 12(4): 35-39.

Wallas, G. (1925). *The art of thought.* New York: Harcourt, Brace, and World.

CHAPTER SIX

Meeting the Needs of Gifted Girls

Gifted girls and young women from all ethnic, geographic, and socioeconomic backgrounds are struggling to realize their potential in school. In *Smart Girls Two: A New Psychology of Girls, Women, and Giftedness,* Kerr states: "A society that wastes female brilliance has made it the norm for gifted women to lead an average life, and gifted women have largely adapted to that norm" (1994, p. 171). Unfortunately, many educators do not fully realize that, without intervention, a large portion of gifted female students never use their abilities. The U.S. Department of Education has reinforced this problem by excluding the special needs of girls as critical to the process of setting a national agenda on education (AAUW 1992).

Therefore, the first step in helping gifted girls must be recognition that they have special, even critical needs and that most of them will not meet the challenges they face at school or in the community without some form of intervention (Smutny 1998). In this chapter I examine the needs of gifted girls, how teachers and parents can identify high potential in this population, and strategies that can effectively address their needs.

Common Problems

The common problems facing gifted girls fall into four broad categories: underachievement, ambivalence, perfectionism, and problems associated with socioeconomic and ethnic factors.

Underachievement. Viewed as a discrepancy between achievement and ability, underachievement afflicts too many gifted girls for anyone to assert that such cases are unique or merely family-related. While women may not experience exclusion from a certain field of study or profession, as they might have in the past, they continue to experience it mentally, socially, and psychologically. These exclusionary feelings begin early in a girl's schooling. Few people today would feel comfortable expressing the sentiments of Euripides (484-406 B.C.), who wrote: "A woman should be good for everything at home, but good for nothing abroad." Yet, as this chapter will demonstrate, female students receive subtle versions of the same message: Avoid math and science (too hard for girls). Don't ask too many questions. Don't put your hand up all the time. Don't be too assertive. Don't . . . . Don't . . . . Don't.

Some teachers assume that giftedness will exempt female students from the deleterious effects of gender bias, but the opposite is true. Female students' exceptional abilities often make them more vulnerable, more sensitive, and thus more responsive to social expectations and limitations than the rest of the population (Silverman 1989). They experience an extraordinary conflict between the drive or hunger to learn and an equally strong desire to make friends and be accepted as a "normal girl" — and not be isolated as a "freak" with her nose in a book.

Such conflicted feelings often are exacerbated by classroom dynamics. Research suggests that, in terms of the quality of their comments, guidance, and suggestions, teachers respond to girls' work with far less care and detail than they do to boys' work. Often they do so without being aware of their actions. Sadker and

Sadker (1994) identified four kinds of teacher response: praise, acceptance, remediation, and criticism. As cited in the AAUW (1992) report,

> They found that while males received more of all four types of teacher comments, the difference favoring boys was greatest in the more useful teacher reactions of praise, criticism, and remediation. When teachers took the time and made the effort to specifically evaluate a student's performance, the student receiving the comment was more likely to be male. (p. 69)

Gifted girls are quick to translate unspoken messages. When a teacher treats a girl as a pushy, impolite or aggressive student (because she asks a lot of questions, often raises her hand, or debates with other students) and rewards a boy for these same behaviors, this teacher is sending a strong message to the class. Gifted girls receive it instantly and often conform to the implied demand (Reis 1990). When a parent encourages a son to follow his interest in math or science but discourages a daughter from doing so, she learns — even at a young age — what subjects are more suitable for girls.

Attempts to moderate or even suppress a girl's passion for learning, combined with the effects of gender stereotyping in the media and peer pressure, foster a low self-image in talented female students. Low self-esteem has been cited as the key reason that talented girls withdraw from more advanced courses in math and science (AAUW 1992). Over time, many gifted girls conform to what others expect from them — to what is considered appropriate for girls to be or do. Underachievement is the result of this process.

Ambivalence. Gifted girls often feel torn between their desire, on one hand, to pursue their talents and interests and their need, on the other hand, to care for and be accepted by others. This ambivalence becomes particularly acute in the middle school and high school years. According to the AAUW (1992) report: "Their responses reveal a sometimes debilitating tension between caring for themselves and caring for others, between their understanding of the world and their awareness that it is not appropriate to speak or act on this understanding" (p. 12). Because of this ambivalence, competitive learning environments can prevent gifted girls from participating fully in any activity that would draw attention to themselves or cause them to surpass a peer (Reis 1998).

Perfectionism. Many gifted children struggle with perfectionism. They typically compound the difficulties of perfectionism with self-esteem problems. Kerr (1994) points out that talented girls often convince themselves that they are "frauds." In consequence, they work harder to hide the fact that they are not what they seem, and this effort results in even greater achievement, which then increases the pressure they feel to cover up their "fraud." This cycle can spiral out of control in some cases, resulting in almost paralyzing fear for the female student: fear that she will be "found out," fear that she will not be able to do the work because she can't even get started, and fear of the shame she will feel when people discover she's not smart after all. In this way, the perfectionism that is common to many high-ability students is compounded by the conviction (among gifted girls) that they are "not really gifted" and therefore must double their efforts to avoid discovery.

Socioeconomic and Ethnic Factors. Socioeconomic status (SES) exerts a powerful influence on the educational development of gifted girls. However, social class, ethnicity, and gender combine in complex ways that make it difficult to detect the needs of gifted girls. Among low-SES eighth-graders, for example, girls test higher than boys in reading and math (AAUW 1992). This changes during the high school years, when boys make significant gains over girls.

Ethnicity and culture also exert specific pressures that affect gifted girls. Latina girls suffer the most dramatic descent in self-esteem. Rarely called on in class and least likely to be identified as gifted, urban Latina girls have a high dropout rate in the United States (Orenstein 1994). African-American girls experience a dual self-image. They do not suffer the same loss in self-esteem between age 11 and 17 as do girls in other groups (Kerr 1994).

Mary Williams Burgher (1979) found that African-American girls — free from the European femininity model of idealized helplessness — are encouraged to measure their worth through strength of character and a tenacious sense of self. However, the nurturing strength that undergirds the growth of African-American girls at home or in their community can dissipate when they enter a predominantly white school. Teachers often reinforce African Americans in certain social behaviors while they reinforce the whites in achievement (AAUW 1992). This is where the "dual self-esteem" asserts itself, making gifted African-American girls feel valued and talented in their private community of friends and family but banished from the privileged domain of academics (Orenstein 1994).

Identification

Gifted girls may be invisible to teachers because teachers often are so burdened with other responsibilities that they can hardly find the time to explore alternative methods for identifying giftedness among special populations. Following are some methods that have proven effective.

Observing Behaviors. Standardized tests may identify some gifted girls, but those with exceptionally low self-esteem or those who have attitudinal or other problems may not perform well on tests. An effective alternative to testing is to observe and document specific behaviors. Following are some general guidelines for discovering talent in gifted girls (Smutny 1998):

First, become familiar with a range of gifted behaviors common in the general population of gifted students. Examples of such behaviors fall into two categories.

Academic Behaviors:

- Reads voraciously and retains what she reads;
- Communicates ideas well both verbally and in writing;
- Possesses superior analytical and conceptual abilities; and
- Explores and synthesizes issues from multiple points of view.

Creative Behaviors:

- Expresses unusual, out-of-the-way points of view;
- Demonstrates special ability in the visual arts;
- Shows promise in performing arts (music, drama, dance); and
- Manifests improvisational ability in a variety of contexts.

Second, become aware of the special challenges that gifted girls face, including:

- Low self-esteem;
- Apathy based on resignation or feelings of inferiority;
- Fear of taking risks;
- Exaggerated concern about acceptance among peers;
- Ambivalent feelings about talent; and
- Conflict between cultural identity and school achievement.

Finally, examine the signs of potential giftedness. While individuals express talent in different ways, common indicators include:

- Discrepancies between performance and self-concept;
- Discrepancies between average or low test scores and exceptional originality, imagination, and insight in independent projects or assignments;
- Disinclination to participate, despite signs of talent or ability;
- Sudden, unaccountable appearance of some ability in a seemingly average girl;
- Misbehavior in class that shows ingenuity (despite its disruptiveness) or that reveals leadership ability; and
- Notable contrast between school performance and the abilities, achievements, and activities reported by parents or community members.

Consulting with Parents. Another way to gauge the potential of gifted girls is to consult with parents. Parents are in the position to detect discrepancies between their daughters' abilities and their achievement in school. Parents often have examples of their children's work at home, such as science projects, artwork, writing samples, and other products. A teacher-parent partnership, in which both adults are sensitive to and aware of the challenges facing gifted girls, can be a powerful support system for a struggling female student. Parents usually know the sorts of activities that make their daughters uncomfortable and may have insights about why they are retreating from their own abilities.

Redesigning the Classroom. Discovering talent in female populations also must involve an awareness of how conventional classrooms discourage these students from performing at their ability level. Instructional methods, teacher-student interactions, curriculum, and the very goals of education often respond more to male than female needs (Shakeshaft 1986). Gilligan's (1982) ground-breaking research on the moral psychology of women and the work of other researchers (for example, Kerr 1994; Orenstein 1994; Sadker and Sadker 1994; Reis 1998; Rimm 1999) have demonstrated how gender bias in our schools inhibits the growth and development of girls. As teachers become more aware of the challenges of gifted girls, begin to reassess their classrooms, and create a wider range of learning options, the potential of gifted girls will become more visible.

Strategies for Nurturing Talent

To create a classroom environment conducive to addressing the educational and emotional needs of gifted girls, teachers can consider the following factors.

Examine Interactions. Gifted girls are sensitive to social interactions with other students as well as to those with the teacher. A first step in improving the classroom environment for gifted girls is to examine the quality of these interactions. What are the underlying expectations? Do girls feel pressured by their peers to "be" a certain way? Does the teacher expect girls to have the same level of intellectual ability in all subjects (including math and science) as boys? Does the teacher respond to girls' questions with the same depth or detail as to boys' questions? Are there any characteristics (assertiveness, unbridled enthusiasm, curiosity and active questioning about many subjects) considered more tolerable in boys than girls? How does gender stereotyping try to manifest itself? Do girls feel free to speak, act, lead as do boys? If not, why not?

Reduce Competition. With some exceptions, gifted girls tend to retreat from highly competitive learning environments. They may perform well, but they do it quietly and often invisibly. Strategies such as learning groups, hands-on activities, and independent projects allow gifted girls to use their talents more freely. These and similar alternative learning structures lessen the conflict they feel between their need to excel and their "ethic of caring" (Gilligan 1982) — their sensitivity to the feelings of others.

Use Clustering. By creating an all-girls cluster of gifted students, teachers provide opportunities for them to advance at their own pace in a comfortable learning environment (Research for Action 1996). The girls can move quickly without worrying about what others will think or feel in response to their performance. For those who doubt their abilities, becoming part of an accepting group of gifted girls may stimulate their interests and help to reverse the negative effects of underachievement.

Use Compacting. The advantage of compacting (discussed in Chapters Three and Four) is that it enables gifted girls to advance at their own pace without drawing attention to themselves (Winebrenner 1992). Many girls feel self-conscious about their abilities and may prefer not to be pulled out for a gifted program. Using learning contracts, teachers can negotiate with gifted girls about alternative work they could do, such as move on to more advanced content within a subject or design a research project that interests them.

Integrate Learning and Thinking Styles. Gifted girls benefit from assignments or activities that combine learning styles (for example, auditory with kinesthetic or visual with linguistic). Using Gardner's (1983) multiple intelligences to broaden the range of learning activities and environments means that gifted girls do not have to compete with peers or to confine themselves to one or two learning styles. An example might be a math class in which students have the option of using art materials to demonstrate their understanding of geometric concepts or an art class in which students investigate effects of the sciences on the arts. Other possibilities include: a gifted writer creating a piece of historical fiction as part of an assignment for a history class; a student with expertise in ornithology making maps and diagrams of migration routes of birds in a geography class. For more ideas on how to use Gardner's intelligences in the classroom, teachers may consult Lazear's *Seven Ways of Knowing* (1991), a comprehensive guide that translates Gardner's intelligences into a wide range of useful techniques and activities.

Organize Girl Groups. Girl groups include any activities, clubs, or classes in which all members are female. Supervised by teachers, counselors, instructional aides, or community volunteers, these groups form around student interests. Questionnaires and informal discussions can generate ideas about the kinds of groups girls would like to join. Groups may range from athletic teams to science or math clubs, art classes, all-girls dramatic clubs or debating teams. These groups are highly beneficial, especially for middle-grades gifted girls who tend to narrow their prospects for the future in response to social pressures (Research for Action 1996).

Arrange Mentorships. "Nothing is more important to girls' developing sense of self than a mentor" (Research for Action 1996, p. 86). This is particularly true in math and science, which girls frequently avoid because of a conviction that classes in these subjects lead them nowhere (Smutny 1998). Professionals in various fields can work with girls in the classroom or involve them in on-site mentoring. However, finding mentors for gifted girls can be difficult. Community contacts and a strong coalition of teachers and parents can be instrumental in locating talent and creating a network that can stimulate and support the talents of gifted girls.

Encourage Leadership. Gifted girls sometimes shy away from leadership roles. They imagine that other students will criticize or resent them, or they fear that they do not have what it takes to lead others. Because of limited socialization, girls in general often lack leadership experience. An effective way to give them this experience is to assign a girl to a temporary leadership position in a group of gifted girls. Telling the group that assigned students are "temporary" leaders and that they will rotate periodically takes the pressure off individual girls. Because the teacher has not selected them above their peers, they can work their way into the new position freely. The teacher assigns the leaders specific responsibilities (for example, taking notes on ideas offered by the group, ensuring that all group members have a chance to speak and that everyone stays focused on the goal of the assignment, and so forth). As girls become more confident, the teacher can increase the challenge. Leaders can tackle more complicated group tasks in which they may have to resolve disputes, inspire disgruntled group members, or help set standards for how the group will achieve its goals.

Another way to give girls experience in leadership is through role-playing simulations. Girls assume roles they may not associate with women (a secret agent, a politician, a soldier, a marine biologist) and take bold actions (challenge a supervisor, give a speech, or arrest a gang of bullies). The fictional elements permit gifted girls to experiment with leadership and assertive behaviors without feeling awkward or timid. The experience provides a safe place to practice more assertive behavior.

Include Women in the Curriculum. The exclusion of women from the curriculum is a factor in girls' diminishing self-esteem (Smutny 1998; Kerr 1994; Martel 1990). Those concerned with curriculum planning for the gifted do not always consider the focus on male achievement (male historical figures, male inventors, male politicians, male artists, male scientists, and so on) at the expense of women and their contributions (McCormick and Wolf 1993). In addition, as Reis (1998) points out, even an emphasis on critical thinking (the most common goal of gifted programs) rests on a concept of logical reasoning and "male orientations to what is fact" (p. 289). Curricula considered appropriate for all gifted children often focus on skills and abilities that have emerged from research on gifted males, not gifted females.

Teachers need to screen their curricula for gender bias — for assumptions about appropriate female activity, distortions that make it appear as though few or no women have made significant contributions to a subject, and stereotypes that reinforce underachievement. Finding role models for a girl interested in mathematics, for example, does not involve scouring history to dig out one or two female mathematicians who have achieved something. As Reis (1998) observes, "The names of the following female mathematicians from previous generations are usually not recognized by boys or girls: Hypatia, Marie Agnesi, Sophie Germain, Evelyn Boyd Granville, Sonya Kovalevskaya, and Mary Somerville" (p. 324). When girls study about women in a wide range of fields, including mathematics or science, they begin to envision new possibilities for themselves and their future.

Providing opportunities to explore gender issues and to investigate the lives of exceptional women is an important dimension of the curriculum for gifted girls. For example, a focus on culture can include an examination of gender roles. The class could investigate such questions as: What are the values in this society that dictate how boys and girls should be and what they can become? What freedoms do men and women have and what constraints? (Can men be dancers? Can women enter politics? What makes the ideal girl in this society? The ideal boy?) Is ours a matriarchal or patriarchal society? Compare other societies with ours. Another possibility is to expose girls to eminent women in fields that interest them. Teachers can involve them in activities such as:

- Writing historical fiction based on an incident in a woman's life;
- Assuming the identity of various women and writing, dramatizing, or be interviewed on the challenges they faced and the process involved in their discoveries and achievements;
- Demonstrating an experiment or discovery contributed by an outstanding woman achiever;

- Creating a list of the qualities that enabled this girl or woman to overcome barriers to achievement. (What were the barriers? How did she overcome them?)

Sources that offer useful research, guidance, and materials for female students can be found by contacting the American Association for University Women (800/225-9998), the National Women's History Project (707/838-0478), Free Spirit Publishing (612/338-2068), and New Moon, which publishes two outstanding magazines for girls (800/381-4743).

Broadening Support

Teachers who are sensitive and sympathetic to the needs of gifted girls may struggle to find the time or energy to respond to them. A useful resource with practical suggestions and ideas on what can be done in schools is *Girls in the Middle: Working to Succeed in Schools,* by Research for Action (1996). A comprehensive study of urban, suburban, and rural schools in the United States, it offers helpful guidance on how to effect reform in the area of gender awareness and intervention. Without an extraordinary amount of funding or external expertise, a small group of teachers, parents, and community members can create beneficial experiences and support systems for gifted girls. Following are some steps that have proven effective.

Create a Coalition to Study the Problem. A coalition of teachers, parents, and other concerned adults can accomplish a great deal by pooling resources, networking, and sharing knowledge and ideas. To be effective, the first step entails a study of the problem. A number of organizations can provide the needed statistics and research. The American Association of University Women has published many studies that apply to almost every kind of school district. Another useful source is the Wellesley College Center for Research on Women, which publishes a bibliography of research on girls in U.S. schools and strategies for reducing underachievement among female students. In addition to print resources, an inservice on gender issues also can inform concerned educators about the special needs of gifted girls. Schools lack information on the problem of underachievement among female students and receive little or no guidance on strategies they can use to address this problem.

After reviewing and discussing the issues raised in the group study, members can then focus on their own community. What are the needs of gifted girls in their school or district? What specific challenges do educators and students face? What research applies to their community and what does not? Based on their study, what information can they use to create reasonable goals that will help their gifted girls?

Involve Parents. Many parents — even highly educated ones — do not realize the extent to which gender bias still constrains the development of girls and young women. After the civil rights movement and the increase in female employment in some fields, it is hard to believe that we still live in a society strapped by gender bias. Following are a few statistics cited by Reis (1998, pp. 29-30), which demonstrate that much remains to be done in this area:

In the 100-year history of the Nobel Prize, only 11 prizes were awarded to women scientists (Marie Curie won two).

Since 1809 only about one in 1,000 patents has been issued to a woman inventor.

Fewer than 5% of the National Academy of Sciences members are women.

In 1996 only four women headed Fortune 1000 companies. Of the 1,000 largest firms in the United States, only 1% of the top five jobs in those corporations were filled by women.

Women constitute less than 12% of the world's parliaments.

Women are drastically underrepresented in major orchestras in the world. Within the 21 highest budgeted orchestras in the United States, there are no female musical directors or conductors in permanent positions.

Of the 185 high-ranking diplomats to the United Nations, only seven are women.

Of the doctorates granted in mathematics in the mid-1990s, 78% were awarded to men; 22% to women. The same percentages held in the physical sciences.

In the House of Representatives, women hold 10.9% of the seats. In the U.S. Senate, women hold 10%.

Only 24 women were elected heads of state or government in the last century.

This list is by no means comprehensive, but it can alert parents to the barriers to achievement that women still face in many arenas. Teachers and parents can discuss these gender issues at parent-teacher conferences and create strategies to help talented girls negotiate some of the challenges they face in school, at home, and in the community.

Explore Community Resources. With a coalition of concerned adults formed to address concerns for the future of gifted girls, members can explore local resources. There is a wide range of possibilities (depending on the community):

- Education professors at nearby institutions who might be interested in doing research on gender in the school;
- Businesses or industries interested in training gifted girls or providing mentors;
- Arts companies willing to do residencies for a group of talented girls;
- Libraries willing to create displays on gender issues and to provide extra reading materials for the school;
- Stores interested in donating materials for specific projects; and
- A group of parents, teachers, and community members willing to develop special projects for gifted girls on subjects that interest them and to pool their own talents and areas of expertise to provide mentorship, instruction, and guidance (ideal in remote communities with few resources).

Each school district has its own culture and its own particular collection of talents, interests, and resources. But in most communities there are people with expertise and business connections who are responsive to the plight of gifted females. Sometimes it pays to extend the definition of community; a "community" resource may be a university 20 miles away or a technology company two towns away. By broadening the network of support, teachers and other concerned adults can develop more services and programs (for example, mentorships, workshops with prominent female professionals, and career counseling sessions) to help gifted girls discover their talents, define their goals, and get the support they need to pursue their true interests.

Advocate for Gifted Girls. A mistake some teachers and parents make is to try to create broad, sweeping changes all at once. This rarely works and can be immensely taxing. Progress usually happens incrementally — in small steps that address one need at a time. Lloyd (1999) cites an example from her experience: She met with a principal to discuss the problem of so few girls taking higher-level math courses. The principal agreed to let Lloyd and several other mothers tutor gifted girls in mathematics to help them overcome their intimidation and disbelief in their ability to do math. Over time, these girls became more confident. Currently, girls are equally represented in the district's high school upper-level math classes. Lloyd offers the following advice to those interested in making positive changes for gifted girls: "One thing I've learned in my years of advocating for students is that getting grand and widespread changes seldom happens. Small and simple changes build and grow. Taken together, eventually they will lead to our reaching larger and loftier goals" (p. 20).

Concluding Thoughts

A significant number of gifted girls camouflage themselves in the classroom and can make their talents appear ordinary or nonexistent. More often than not, they do so without knowing they are doing it. And they do it because they have learned not to pose a threat to anyone, not to be too aggressive about what they know or want to know, and because they do not want their abilities to endanger relationships they value. Research on girls' school experiences clearly demonstrates that the education system is teaching students more than academic subjects. Like other channels for information in our society (popular media, peers, family, and so on), schools prepare children for gender roles. For gifted girls, such preparation often means schooling them for underachievement.

Girls with special talents need classrooms in which the freedom to explore their interests and strengths is strong and teachers consistently validate their gifts and understand their sensibilities. In any given class today, girls gifted in math, science, the arts, or the humanities sit quietly in their seats, trying not to draw attention to themselves. How many of these high-potential students discover their greatest strengths and passions is unknown. What is known is that teachers and parents who choose to advocate for gifted girls — to become informed counselors, mentors, and nurturers — play a significant role in the growth and development of gifted girls.

Notes

American Association of University Women (AAUW). (1992). *How schools shortchange girls.* Washington, D.C.: American Association of University Women Educational Foundation.

Burgher, M.W. (1979). Images of self and race in the autobiographies of black women. In R.P. Bell, B.J. Parker, and B.Guy-Sheftall (Eds.), *Sturdy black bridges: Visions of black women in literature.* New York: Anchor.

Gardner, H. (1983). *Frames of mind.* New York: Basic Books.

Gilligan, C. (1982). *In a different voice.* Cambridge, Mass.: Harvard University Press.

Kerr, B.A. (1994). *Smart girls two: A new psychology of girls, women, and giftedness.* Dayton, Ohio: Psychology Press.

Lazear, D. (1991). *Seven ways of knowing: Teaching for multiple intelligences.* 2nd ed. Palatine, Ill.: Skylight.

Lloyd, M. (1999). Carousel . . . girls and the M word. *Understanding Our Gifted* 11(2): 19-20.

Martel, A. (1990). Pedagogic interventions for gifted girls and women. In J.L. Ellis and J.M. Willinsky (Eds.), *Girls, women, and giftedness.* Monroe, N.Y.: Trillium.

McCormick, M.E., and Wolf, J.S. (1993). Intervention programs for gifted girls. *Roeper Review* 16 (December): 85-88.

Orenstein, P., in association with the American Association of University Women. (1994). *Schoolgirls: Young women, self-esteem, and the confidence gap.* New York: Doubleday.

Reis, S.M. (1990). We can't change what we don't recognize: Understanding the special needs of gifted females. In J.L Ellis and J.M. Willinsky (Eds.), *Girls, women, and giftedness.* Monroe, N.Y.: Trillium.

Reis, S.M. (1998). *Work left undone: Choices and compromises of talented females.* Mansfield Center, Conn.: Creative Learning.

Research for Action. (1996). *Girls in the middle: Working to succeed in school.* Washington, D.C.: American Association of University Women Educational Foundation.

Rimm, S. (1999). *See Jane win: The Rimm report on how 1,000 girls became successful women.* New York: Crown.

Sadker, M. and Sadker, D. (1994). *Failing at fairness: How America's schools cheat girls.* New York: Charles Scribner's Sons.

Shakeshaft, C. (1986). A gender at risk. *Phi Delta Kappan* 67(7): 499-508.

Silverman, L.K. (1989). Reclaiming lost giftedness in girls. *Understanding Our Gifted* 2 (November-December): 7-9.

Smutny, J.F. (1998). *Gifted girls.* (Fastback 427). Bloomington, Ind.: Phi Delta Kappa Educational Foundation.

Winebrenner, S. (1992). *Teaching gifted kids in the regular classroom.* Minneapolis, Minn.: Free Spirit.

CHAPTER SEVEN

Culturally Different and Disadvantaged Gifted Children

A review of research on giftedness over the past 50 years will quickly reveal that most studies have focused on children from white, middle-class culture. The understanding of intelligence and giftedness that evolved, therefore, was specific to the culture that ruled American society. The results speak for themselves. Researchers have estimated the underrepresentation of minority students in gifted programs to be anywhere from 30% to 70% (Richert 1987). During the 1980s, a report from the U.S. Department of Education noted that the percentage of minorities in gifted programs (with the exception of Asians) falls far below the percentage in total school enrollment (Barstow 1987). The Ross Report (Ross 1993) stated that a meager 9% of the students in gifted programs came from families in the bottom income quartile, which includes a large number of minority populations; 47% came from the top (predominantly white) quartile.

Despite an increase in interest and concern for these populations, the problems remain: deeply entrenched beliefs about intelligence that discriminate against the culturally different and that limit the kinds of abilities considered "gifted," little public understanding of and experience in giftedness among other cultural groups, no recognition of their special educational needs, no consensus at the policy level to tackle the problem of severe underachievement among the gifted from minority groups, and limited resources and funding to meet these needs.

Cultural Bias in Testing

One of the first obstacles that gifted minority students face is inherent cultural bias in the standardized testing system. Baldwin (1987) points out that IQ cut-off scores disqualify a significant portion of gifted minority children at the outset. Bernal (2003) also attributes the gross underrepresentation of culturally different children in gifted programs to current screening practices, which are largely dependent on test scores.

The genesis of the testing movement in this country laid the foundation for cultural bias. During the early part of the 20th century, influential researchers, such as Terman and Brigham, were focusing on the distribution of intelligence among the races and reported lower IQs among African-American, Spanish, Indian, and Eastern European groups (see Kamin 1974). As members of the eugenics movement, they concluded that discrepancies between the test scores of whites and other groups could be explained only by race or nationality. Their "findings" had a political dimension: Establishing genetic inferiority justified the Johnson-Lodge Immigration Act of 1924, which limited the immigration of groups considered mentally deficient. Walter Lippmann foresaw the threat that testing posed to social justice and equal access to opportunity:

> If the tester would make good his claim, he would soon
> occupy a position of power which no intellectual has held

since the collapse of theocracy. The vista is intoxicating enough. . . . The unconscious temptation is too strong for the ordinary critical defenses of the scientific methods. (in Gould 1981, p. 180)

Until the 1960s and 1970s few voices spoke out against cultural bias in testing (Samuda 1975). In 1968 the Association of Black Psychologists reacted against the ethnocentric nature of standardized measurements and declared a moratorium on testing (p. 4). Culture-sensitive educators began to challenge a number of assumptions:

- The assumption that only the mainstream definition of intelligence is valid;
- The assumption that the small percentage of the minority gifted programs is due to the low incidence of giftedness in these populations; and
- The assumption that tests can actually measure the whole of individual mental ability and that once cultural bias is extracted from an instrument, it can accurately assess a student's "innate" intelligence.

These ideas began to give way to new assumptions as a result of the innovative work of researchers, including Bruch (1975), Torrance (1977), Bernal (1981), Frasier (1981), and Sisk (1981), who felt that identifying giftedness within other cultures must involve consulting the definitions of talent and ability within those cultures. The mainstream concept of intelligence became suspect not only because of its cultural biases but also because of its oversimplified view of human potential. This view lent support to the IQ test that provided a way to quantify ability — to convert the complexity of human intelligence into a simple number. The schools needed a "scientific" method they could use to justify program decisions for students, and the testing industry made extraordinary gains in prestige and profit from reinforcing the validity and reliability of standardized testing.

Spanning the last 30 years, the new testing movement has tried to remedy bias related to such factors as language differences, ethnocentric test items, inappropriate norm sampling, and issues of test administration (time limits, lack of motivation, test anxiety, and so on). The Rural and Migrant Gifted Project (Ortiz and Gonzalez 1991) created a model for identifying gifted Latino students that included a shortened version of the Wechsler Intelligence Scale for Children-Revised (WISC-R) in both English and Spanish (Ortiz and Gonzalez 1989). The instructions and time limits were adjusted, and specific items were replaced with more culturally appropriate ones. The Abbreviated Binet for the Disadvantaged, Raven Progressive Matrices Test, and the System of Multicultural Pluralistic Assessment (SOMPA), Structure of the Intellect-Learning Abilities (SOI-LA), and the Torrance Tests of Creative Thinking all responded in varying degrees to the need for tests sensitive to the special environmental and cultural differences of disadvantaged and culturally different groups. Many of these instruments use a variety of approaches to measure potential in the cognitive, psychosocial, psychomotor, creative, and task-commitment domains. For example, the SOI-LA uses Guilford's model to produce a profile of a child's intellectual processes. It stresses figural rather than verbal abilities.

The new Raven Progressive Matrices Test, revised in 1998, is a nonreading test and allows children to use their strengths — whether they be visual or verbal — to complete tasks. As a self-teaching instrument that does not rely on past exposure to subject matter, the Raven also provides a more level playing field.

The focus of psychometrics has shifted from testing for prediction to testing for description (Samuda 1975); from identifying the weaknesses of other cultures and economic groups to identifying their strengths; from perceiving a deficit in minority children to perceiving a difference. The impetus of this movement sought to respond in practical terms to the question: "How can we stem the waste of human potential and bring hope and motivation where frustration and despair exist?" (Samuda 1975, p. 151).

Alternative Selection Methods

Pioneers in gifted education saw that the only way to reverse the trend of neglect was to make the identification process more multifaceted and less test-bound and to make standardized test scores only one of a number of equally weighted criteria. Almost two decades after the Marland report (see Chapter One) provided an official definition of giftedness for the United States, another report by the Department of Education defined giftedness in intellectual, creative, and artistic terms and recognized special abilities in leadership and a number of specific fields (Ross 1993). The Ross Report further established that giftedness is a phenomenon occurring in *all* cultures and economic strata. By confirming the pioneering work of intelligence researchers such as Guilford and his Structure of the Intellect Model, which established as many as 120 factors in cognitive functioning, the Ross Report dispelled the notion of intelligence as a single, quantifiable entity represented by an IQ score.

Matrix identification models use a variety of sources to gather information on potentially gifted minority students, including areas in which giftedness would most likely appear in specific cultures. An example of this type of model is the Kranz Talent Identification Instrument (Kranz 1981), designed specifically for culturally diverse and poor gifted children. Another is the Baldwin Identification Matrix (Baldwin 1978), which draws on objective and subjective criteria and has increased the number of African-American students in gifted programs. Although not technically a matrix model, Torrance's (1977) research on "creative positives" includes a wide range of cognitive and improvisational abilities among non-mainstream populations and explores other criteria for assessing giftedness. Educators can use his list of "positives" as a guide to observing and documenting behaviors.

Alternative assessment practices almost always involve a direct experience of a child's work either through observation, informal interview, or activities designed to demonstrate particular abilities. Sisk (1981), in her work with poor, culturally different students, identified the gifted by using theater techniques, cultural positives (Torrance 1977), and the ABDA (Abbreviated Binet) to gain a more comprehensive picture of each child's ability. In Connecticut the Encendiendo Uno Llama programs used a multiple-criteria process to identify gifted bilingual students based on trial participation and firsthand examination of students' work (Barstow 1987). Gay (1978) describes a plan for identifying gifted African-American students using individual conferences in which candidates share their work through a demonstration or presentation and engage in group problem-solving activities to demonstrate organizational and leadership abilities. The DISCOVER assessment process (Nielson 2001; Maker 1996) at the University of Arizona has capitalized on Gardner's theory of multiple intelligences and focused on how children engage in the complex behavior of solving problems and creating products. The assessment process occurs in the regular classroom with students in small groups using the language of their preference, while observers move from group to group recording the behaviors that the children exhibit while solving problems. Each child is assessed by several observers in a variety of activities and using different "intelligences."

Drawing, in part, from Renzulli's three-ring theory of intelligence (1977), Baldwin (2001) proposed a broad definition of giftedness as shown in high general ability, task commitment, and creative problem-solving in a wider range of domains — cognitive, psychosocial, psychomotor, or creative (visual or performing arts). She established alternative assumptions to guide the identification and education of gifted among low socioeconomic and culturally different communities:

- Giftedness can be expressed through a variety of behaviors.
- Giftedness expressed in one area (as just listed) is just as important as giftedness expressed in another.
- Giftedness in any area can be a clue to the presence of potential giftedness in another area, or a catalyst for the development of giftedness in another area.

- A total ability profile is crucial in planning an educational program for gifted children.
- All populations have gifted children who exhibit behaviors that are indicative of giftedness. (Baldwin 2003, p. 86)

In this time of school reform and increased public criticism of inequities in the educational services provided to students, more action research projects have focused on improving selection methods for culturally different students. Participating universities of the National Research Center on the Gifted and Talented (NRC/GT) have successfully implemented many of the ideas discussed in this chapter. In particular, researchers found nontraditional methods critical to gaining a complete profile of high-ability minority children (Callahan, Tomlinson, and Pizzat 1994). Examples of these methods include: art tasks, essays, hands-on problem-solving activities, videotaped sessions documenting gifted behaviors, checklists, interviews, and portfolios of the children's work. What researchers have learned through these approaches have led to the development of more appropriate programming.

Minority Gifted Programs:
Assimilation Versus Cultural Pluralism

Philosophical approaches to the education of gifted minority students fall roughly into two categories. One side contends that only through assimilation will minority talent thrive. This side claims that cultural values tend to separate children from mainstream society and thus obstruct their access to educational and other opportunities (Banks 1979). The opposing side insists that learning how to function effectively in mainstream culture should never require imitation. Cultural strengths, far from disabling minority students, empower them to achieve and should be at the heart of any program for gifted, culturally different students (Torrance 1977; Rimm 1987; Ford, Grantham, and Harris 1997; Sisk 2001; Bernal 2003).

While the dust over this debate is far from settled, assimilation has not become a proven method of educating the culturally different. In the process of acquiring the skills, knowledge, and culture of mainstream America, many students experience a sense of isolation from their own community. They gain access to more opportunities, both educational or professional. But they often feel a distance between themselves and peers and may learn to devalue their culture. (Children who refuse to speak their native tongue or disparage local traditions are examples of this phenomenon).

Cultural pluralists are quick to weigh the gains of their approach against the losses. What does a child sacrifice in the process of imitating the majority culture? The message to the child is: "To succeed with us, you must be like us." The message to the child's community is: "You are keeping this child back." However sensitive their teachers or program directors may be, the children cannot avoid the sense of lack and deficiency that underlie an assimilationist program's approach. The family cannot avoid it either. Davis and Rimm (1994) note that parents will support special programs only if these programs understand their children's special gifts, recognize the opportunities available to gifted students, and learn that these programs will not alienate their children from them or their community.

Cultural Strengths

In recent years some researchers have suggested that gifted education, with its unfortunate reputation as "elitist," would do well to participate in the country's reform agenda by shifting gifted education into a multicultural mode (Ford, Grantham, and Harris 1997). Along similar lines, Bernal (1998; 2003) suggests creating a "transitional" bilingual program for gifted students that would capitalize on their abilities in their native language and include multicultural education as a preparation for a regular, multicultural gifted program. Bernal's proposal is a radical departure from the remedial model commonly used for culturally different students, particularly English-learners. Schools often assume that bilingual children need to master English *before* receiving a more challenging academic and creative education (Kitano and Espinosa 1995). Such entrenched attitudes about culturally different children would punish gifted students for speaking another language or, in the case of low-income children, for living in a poor neighborhood.

Scruggs and Cohn (1983) described a Native American child who had exceptional gifts, yet was deficient in academic skill areas. These authors developed an individualized program that capitalized on the student's talents and interests to help him develop skill and knowledge. Because of the open-ended nature of his program, he improved rapidly in skill areas and discovered new abilities and interests. His mentors placed him at advantage, rather than disadvantage.

In places where a large number of children from a particular culture live, programs can use specific cultural values, traditions, and materials to structure content. An excellent example is the Na Pua No'Eau program model in Hawaii (Martin, Sing, and Hunter 2003). Na Pua refers to flowers (the children of Hawaii) and No'Eau to the talents that blossom in the process of self-discovery. A solidly multicultural program, this model integrates Hawaiian ideas about talent and identity development, Hawaiian values and traditions, and the central role of family and community with Western methods for study, exploration, and enrichment. Gifted students who have benefited from the program find they can advance themselves in subjects they particularly enjoy — such as marine biology — while also exploring their Hawaiian heritage. For children not raised in the traditional Hawaiian way, the cultural dimension of the program increases positive feelings about who they are and what they have to contribute *as Hawaiians.*

Culturally different and disadvantaged gifted students need to engage in complex content and thinking processes that draw on multiple intelligences, to work in an interdisciplinary mode and in an environment that incorporates multicultural resources and practices, and to use preferred learning styles. Gardner's (1983) theory of multiple intelligences, Guilford's (1967) Structure of the Intellect Model, Renzulli's (1977) Enrichment Triad Model, and other models have provided conceptual and practical guides for designing appropriate curriculum. Maker and Nielson (1996) recommend the following modifications in the learning environment to accommodate culturally different gifted children:

- Learner-centered rather than teacher-centered;
- Independence rather than dependence on teacher's direction;
- Openness to new ideas and approaches rather than closed;
- Acceptance of ideas for discussion rather than premature judgment;
- Complexity of content designed to stimulate application of new information;
- Variety of grouping options for all activities;
- Flexibility in structure of planned activities; and
- High mobility in the classroom encouraged.

The curriculum of Project, a three-week intensive gifted summer program at National-Louis University, which I developed, embodies a number of these modifications. It features hands-on projects that allow for multiple learning styles, high mobility between small-group and independent work, and focus on discovery, invention, and creativity. An economics class had students assume the roles of business leaders, investors, consumers, and workers through a series of simulations. Over the three weeks, the class grappled with the intriguing relationships between money supply, inflation, the GNP, the national debt, and unemployment. In a class on mathematical curves, students progressed from an exploration of the simplest circles to the trigonometric function curves and exotic cycloid and spiral curves. Finding curves in spider webs, sound waves, and galaxies, as demonstrated in class activities, inspired many children who might ordinarily lose interest in abstract mathematical thinking. Having the class explore modern mathematical applications in the Golden Gate Bridge or automobile headlights further expanded course content for students with limited experience in algebra. In an aquatic biology class, students tested water samples and researched ecological problems in their areas.

In visual and performing arts classes, students used their creative strengths to design unique performances or products and explore modes of self-expression through a wide range of media. Culturally different students, who might cringe before pen and paper assignments, wrote furiously for three weeks in an open-ended creative writing class in which they responded to a wide range of catalysts — from films to photographs and paintings — to create material for poems, stories, and essays. They assembled a 200-page illustrated, creative writing magazine.

If these students had attended formal academic classes emphasizing a purely abstract, linear approach through the lecture method, they might have revealed only moderate talent. Culturally different children need opportunities to express their strengths — their improvisational powers, their quick verbal wit, their analytical and problem-solving abilities, their inventive spirit, and creative thinking.

Parent and Community Involvement

The role of parents in the development of gifted children can never be over-emphasized. Davis and Rimm (1994) state that high-achieving gifted, culturally different students tend to have parents who provide plenty of encouragement, affection, and interest; establish high (but not unreasonable) goals of performance; and maintain strong communication to encourage their independence and productivity. Frasier (1981) emphasizes the value of parental involvement and counseling and suggests decision-making strategies such as "futuring" (projecting oneself into the future), mental imagery, and guided fantasy to help gifted minority students explore alternative careers.

Pluralist programs try to consult with parents about the talents of their children and their education needs and with community people who can be counselors and colleagues to support the students' forward steps. Programs such as Project STEP-UP (Sisk 1981; 2003), which involved 14 districts in four states and three universities, have made extensive use of parent and community contact in their work with minority gifted students. As an early intervention program, Project STEP-UP requires active parent involvement and support. The Project (at National-Louis University) gives parent seminars on identifying and understanding giftedness in their children. Parents of students in the Na Pua No'Eau Program participate in workshops that re-connect them to Hawaiian values and enhance their understanding of their children's gifts. The program consistently uses parents and community members as volunteers and sources of knowledge.

Pluralist programs also use community members to help them find gifted children, learn more about the different talents valued by other cultures, function as counselors to gifted students, assist or teach in classes (particularly where a second language is involved), and help maintain links between the program and students' families.

In the three-week program of the Project, which I developed at National-Louis University, families and community organizers advised program staff about the needs of the children and their learning styles. Liaisons and teaching colleagues were crucial communicators for parents and students through the three weeks and kept the staff informed about students' progress and problems. Parents attended the open house and observed their children in action — on the dance floor, on stage, in the laboratory, in print. Teachers shared specific suggestions about resources for their children during the year. Follow-up sessions through the year served to keep many parents and community people current about career facts, schools, and universities. A wide variety of professionals helped to dislodge some deep-seated misconceptions about what sorts of careers are "appropriate" or "realistic" for culturally different populations.

Without the crucial component of parent involvement, culturally different children often withdraw from the program because of family resistance to something they do not understand. Rather than wait until some problem or misunderstanding arises, teachers and administrators need to make parents a vital part of the program. If parents and communities have an investment in the program and own it, others will follow. The program becomes something they take pride in, rather than something that separates them from their children.

Looking Ahead

Even with all of the research and labor of concerned educators, minority and disadvantaged gifted students still lag far behind their white, middle-class counterparts. Shaklee and Hamilton (2003) point out that despite expanded views of intelligence brought about by many researchers, including Gardner (1983), Gagné (1995), Feldhusen (1992), and others, most school programs still identify gifted children through traditional tests. A large number of these neglected students are culturally different as well as disadvantaged and, as our education system stands now, they have little chance of discovering their abilities or benefiting from any special services for gifted students. Research and innovative programming efforts have not resulted in fundamental changes for culturally different gifted children on the ground.

There are many reasons why this is so. Selection procedures in schools need a complete overhaul in order to detect giftedness in students from minority cultures or low socioeconomic conditions. Nielson (2003) offers perhaps one of the most comprehensive examples of assessment in the DISCOVER model, using multiple intelligences, problem-solving activities, and direct observations to find gifted children in culturally different populations. Likewise, programming ideas have advanced markedly over the past two decades. More programs are exploring the possibilities of a multicultural modality, such as those that Ford, Grantham and Harris (1997) and Bernal (2003) have proposed. Certainly the Na Pua No'Eau model stands as a clear example of the power this approach offers to culturally different students who entertain doubts about the worth of their culture and the potential of their future in mainstream society.

Ramirez (2003) argues that three main obstacles remain for economically disadvantaged children — and this also applied to culturally different:

- The general orientation of the policy apparatus and the education system toward poor children;
- The societal view of the poor, immigrants, and children of color relative to their educational needs; and

- State funding policies for gifted education programs. (p. 134)

Federal policy, with its focus on the deficits or needs of this population, perpetuates a delivery model that is not constituted to recognize or serve gifted children. Where programs for the gifted exist, many tend to weed out students who do not meet the narrow criteria established. To some extent, it rests with federal and state governments to shift public perceptions and attitudes about culturally different and poor populations and to generate a strong consensus on developing gifted children's talents. Without a fundamental change in how the public perceives the needs of these gifted students, educators can make few improvements in assessment, intervention, and policy.

Concluding Thoughts

Talented culturally different children have stirred up old ways of thinking in gifted education. Their differences question white, middle-class definitions and values that have excluded so many students from other cultures and socioeconomic backgrounds. Talented minorities have a twofold challenge. On the one hand, they need to achieve within the dominant culture in order to grow and contribute. On the other hand, they want to maintain the cultural distinction that differentiates them from the white, middle-class world. For a long time, mainstream society simply excluded them from the wealth of resources available to white students. Then it conceded that minorities could join the ranks of professions formerly reserved for the dominant culture, but only by imitation and assimilation.

Now, more and more, society is including culturally different groups on those groups' own terms. On some level, these groups remind mainstream society of what it lacks and what other cultures can contribute if they have the chance to do so. Given the mounting challenges that can be answered only by inspired, creative thinkers, gifted educators cannot afford to overlook the tragic loss of hidden potential lying waste in many minority communities.

Notes

Baldwin, A.Y. (1978). The Baldwin identification matrix. In A.Y. Baldwin, G.H. Gear, and L.J. Lucito (Eds.), *Educational planning for the gifted: Overcoming cultural, geographic, and socioeconomic barriers.* Reston, Va.: Council for Exceptional Children.

Baldwin, A.Y. (1987). Undiscovered diamonds: The minority gifted child. *Journal for the Education of the Gifted* 10(4): 271-285.

Baldwin, A.Y. (2003). Lost and found: Achievers in urban schools. In J.F. Smutny (Ed.), *Underserved gifted populations: Responding to their needs and abilities* (pp. 83-91). Cresskill, N.J.: Hampton.

Banks, W. (1979). *Teaching strategies for ethnic studies.* 2nd ed. Boston: Allyn and Bacon.

Barstow, D. (1987). Serve disadvantaged and serve all gifted. *Gifted Child Monthly* 8(10): 1-3.

Bernal, E.M. (2003). Delivering two-way bilingual immersion programs to the gifted and talented: A classic yet progressive option for the new millennium. In J.F. Smutny (Ed.), *Underserved gifted populations: Responding to their needs and abilities* (pp. 141-56). Cresskill, N.J.: Hampton.

Bernal, E.M. (1998). Could gifted English language learners save gifted and talented programs in an age of reform and inclusion? *TEMPO* 18(1): 11-14.

Bernal, E.M. (1981). Special problems and procedures for identifying minority gifted students. Paper presented at the Council for Exceptional Children Conference on the Exceptional Bilingual Child, New Orleans, La.

Bruch, C.B. (1975). Assessment of creativity in culturally different children. *Gifted Child Quarterly* 19: 164-74.

Callahan, C.; Tomlinson, C.A.; and Pizzat, P.M. (1994). *Contexts for promise: Noteworthy practices and innovations in the identification of gifted students.* (To order, contact: National Research Center on the Gifted and Talented, University of Virginia, Curry School of Education, 405 Emmet Street, Room 263, Ruffner Hall, Charlottesville, VA 22903).

Davis, G.A., and Rimm, S. B. (1994). *Education of the gifted and talented.* 3rd ed. Boston: Allyn and Bacon.

Feldhusen, J.H. (1992). *Talent identification and development in education (TIDE).* Sarasota, Fla.: Center for Creative Learning.

Ford, D.Y.; Grantham, T.C.; and Harris, J.J., III. (1997). The recruitment and retention of minority teachers in gifted education. *Roeper Review* 19(4): 213-220.

Frasier, M.M. (1981). Minority gifted children. In B.S. Miller and M. Price (Eds.), *The gifted child, the family, and the community.* New York: Walker.

Gagné, F. (1995). From giftedness to talent: A developmental model and its impact on the language of the field. *Roeper Review* 18(2): 103-11.

Gardner, H. (1983). *Frames of mind.* New York: Basic Books.

Gay, J.E. (1978). A proposed plan for identifying black gifted children. *Gifted Child Quarterly* 22: 353-360.

Gould, S.J. (1981). *The mismeasure of man.* New York: W.W. Norton.

Guilford, J.P. (1967). *The nature of human intelligence.* New York: McGraw Hill.

Kamin, L.J. (1974). *The science and politics of IQ.* Potomac, Md.: Lawrence Erlbaum.

Kitano, M.K., and Espinosa, R. (1995). Language diversity and giftedness: Working with gifted English language learners. *Journal for the Education of the Gifted* 18(3): 234-254.

Kranz, B. (1981). *Kranz talent identification instrument.* Moorehead, Minn.: Moorehead State College.

Maker, C.J. (1996). Identification of gifted minority students: A national problem, needed changes, and a promising solution. *Gifted Child Quarterly* 40(1): 41-50.

Maker, C.J., and Nielson, A.B. (1996). *Curriculum development and teaching strategies for gifted learners.* Austin, Tex.: Pro-Ed.

Martin, D.E.; Sing, D.K.; and Hunter, L.A. (2003). Na Pua No'Eau: The Hawaiian perspective of giftedness. In J.F. Smutny (Ed.), *Underserved gifted populations: Responding to their needs and abilities.* (pp. 179-203). Cresskill, N.J.: Hampton.

Nielson, A.B. (2003). The DISCOVER assessment and curriculum models. In J.F. Smutny (Ed.), *Underserved gifted populations: Responding to their needs and abilities.* (pp. 205-37). Cresskill, N.J.: Hampton.

Ortiz, V.Z., and Gonzalez, A. (1989). A validation study of a WISC-R short form with accelerated and gifted Hispanic students. *Gifted Child Quarterly* 33: 152-155.

Ortiz, V.Z., and Gonzalez, A. (1991). Gifted Hispanic adolescents. In M. Birely and J. Genshaft (Eds.), *Understanding the gifted adolescent: Educational, developmental, and multicultural issues* (pp. 240-47). New York: Teachers College Press.

Ramirez, A. (2003). Gifted and poor: America's quiet crisis. In J.F. Smutny (Ed.), *Underserved gifted populations: Responding to their needs and abilities.* (pp. 129-38). Cresskill, N.J.: Hampton.

Renzulli, J.S. (1977). *The enrichment triad model: A guide for developing defensible programs for the gifted and talented.* Mansfield, Conn.: Creative Learning.

Richert, E.S. (1987). Rampant problems and promising practices in the identification of disadvantaged gifted students. *Gifted Child Quarterly* 31: 149-54.

Rimm, S.B. (1987). Creative underachievers: Marching to the beat of a different drummer. *Gifted Child Today* (November-December): 2-6.

Ross, P. (1993). *National excellence: A case for developing America's talent.* Washington, D.C.: U.S. Department of Education, Office of Educational Research and Improvement.

Samuda, R.J. (1975). *Psychological testing of American minorities: Issues and consequences.* New York: Dodd, Mead.

Scruggs, T.E., and Cohn, S.J. (1983). A university-based summer program for a highly able but poorly achieving Indian child. *Gifted Child Quarterly* 27: 90-93.

Shaklee, B.D., and Hamilton, A. (2003). Urban gifted youth. In J.F. Smutny (Ed.), *Underserved gifted populations: Responding to their needs and abilities.* (pp. 93-115).

Sisk, D. (2003). Maximizing the high potential of minority economically disadvantaged students. In J.F. Smutny (Ed.), *Underserved gifted populations: Responding to their needs and abilities.* (pp. 239-59). Cresskill, N.J.: Hampton.

Sisk, D. (1981). The challenge of educating the gifted among the poor. In A.H. Kramer et al. (Ed.), *Gifted children: Challenging their potential—New perspectives and alternatives.* New York: Trillium.

Torrance, E.P. (1977). *Discovery and nurturance of giftedness in the culturally different.* Reston, Va.: Council for Exceptional Children.

CHAPTER EIGHT

Underachievement Among the Gifted

Research has estimated that about half of all identified gifted students underachieve in U.S. schools (National Commission on Excellence in Education 1984; Richert, 1991). A report by the Department of Education (Ross 1993) called the low achievement of so many able children a "quiet crisis." This estimate is especially troubling as it does not include the thousands of gifted students who remain unidentified because of poverty and cultural difference (see Peterson 1999).

It could be argued that the "quiet" of this crisis has perpetuated widespread neglect of America's talent in all sectors of society. Gifted students who do not perform well in school rarely arouse much concern. All schools have children who seem unmotivated, resistant to class activities, or disinclined to apply themselves. The chief difficulty in identifying gifted underachievers lies in their deceptive appearance: Most of them look like average or below-average students.

In this chapter I will explore the factors that make this crisis a "quiet" one: little awareness of gifted underachievers and their problems in school and little or no understanding of how to identify or serve them. I also will examine the most effective strategies for helping such students overcome obstacles to their growth and success and reverse the course of their underachievement.

Underachievement Defined

Achievement in school often defines a gifted child, and so some educators may find the concept of gifted *underachievement* baffling. In addition, schools tend to see special services for the gifted as a reward — something earned by students who have consistently applied themselves and done well (Peterson 2003). Even gifted educators who recognize the diversity and range of giftedness often look for behaviors that underachievers lack, such as high motivation and task commitment.

High ability does not always result in high achievement, which is a critical point for educators to grasp in order to understand this phenomenon. Interestingly, the federal definition of giftedness (Marland 1972) — long used as a standard for identifying eligible students for special programs — tacitly recognized underachievers by including "potential ability" as well as "demonstrated achievement." While schools embraced, and still embrace, this national definition, they tend to exclude gifted children who underachieve — those whose "potential ability" does not bring "demonstrated achievement" in the classroom (Hansford 2003).

Finding this discrepancy between ability and performance is the challenge facing schools. Some educators assume that test scores or other measures can settle the question of underachievers' abilities. But research shows that while testing may be the means to identify some (Peterson 2003), it fails to identify others (Davis and Rimm 1994). Gifted underachievers often do not function well under pressure, particularly in timed situations. Rimm has developed several measures to help teachers identify children that teachers suspect may be gifted underachievers (see

Rimm 1986a; 1987; 1988). To discover more of these under-served students, school districts need to challenge the belief that giftedness can be found only in "demonstrated achievement" and include "potential ability" in identification practices (Gallagher 1985).

Common Characteristics

While underachievement is a diverse phenomenon with unique circumstances attending each case, there are broad categories that can help identify its more common features. Whitmore (1989) found three general categories of underachieving gifted children: those who underachieve because they lack the motivation to apply themselves in school; those whose environments do not nurture their gifts and may even discourage high achievement; and those who have disabilities or learning deficits that mask their giftedness. Despite crucial differences among individual underachievers, a significant number of them respond to similar challenges in similar ways. Commonly cited characteristics of underachieving gifted students include (Davis and Rimm 1994; Van Tassel-Baska 1992; Baum, Owen, and Dixon 1991; Rimm 1986b; Whitmore 1986):

- low self-esteem (this characteristic exists in practically all underachievers)
- negative attitude toward school and learning
- disinclination to take risks when presented with new challenges
- incomplete and poor execution of class work
- strength in imagination and creative activities
- low tolerance for drill work
- weakness in skill areas and organization
- tendency to be distracted
- discomfort with competition
- lack of perseverance
- lack of goal-directed behavior
- social isolation

- acute sensitivity about self and relationships to others
- tendency to disrupt class and resist activities

Rimm (Davis and Rimm 1994) sees characteristics of under-achievers in terms of three distinct levels. Low self-esteem, she argues, is the primary characteristic and the cause of most under-achievement problems. From this primary level emerges a sec-ondary level ("academic avoidance behaviors") that, in turn, leads to tertiary traits: "poor study habits, unmastered skills, and social and discipline problems" (p. 286). Each level supports the one that comes after it.

Low self-esteem — the most common trait among under-achievers (Rimm 1986b; 1995; Whitmore 1980) — arises from a variety of sources. For some, the very pressure of being gifted, especially the fear of disappointing parents with high expecta-tions, may drive a child to underachieve. For other students, a creative and nontraditional learning style coupled with poor organization may make them feel out of sync with the rest of the class. When they fail repeatedly to perform well in ordinary school tasks, their sense of inadequacy increases. Still others may underachieve because of environmental factors, such as poverty, ethnic or racial prejudice, or different cultural values (see Chapter Seven). In each case of underachievement, low self-esteem is tied to specific circumstances that require close analysis to determine an appropriate response.

Secondary characteristics of underachievement refer to a child's "nonproductive avoidance behaviors" (Davis and Rimm 1994, p. 286). Such behaviors enable the student to protect him- or herself for a time. For example, the student may excuse poor work by saying that school has no relevance or, "If I studied or were interested, I could do well." The student may get involved in so many outside activities or interests that there is no time to do school work and in this way avoid the fear of failing. Other secondary characteristics, such as perfectionism, serve a similar purpose. A perfectionist creates such inordinately high expecta-tions that he or she has a constant excuse for not achieving them.

Such students create — in their own minds and in communications with others — a mountain to climb that is so high that anyone will understand if the peak cannot be achieved. Perfectionists often procrastinate or feel paralyzed with fear, either of which enables them to avoid doing what they think will expose them to failure.

Rimm sees secondary characteristics in terms of dependent or dominant defense mechanisms (2003). The "dependent" underachievers have learned to ask help from adults to such an extent that they lose self-confidence, attempt less on their own, and become anxious. The more "dominant" ones choose to do only what they feel confident attempting. They rebel, argue with adults, and see the world around them in an adversarial way. These underachievers experience moments of confidence only when they get what they want from adults.

At the third level of underachievement, the characteristics function to reinforce the general pattern (Davis and Rimm 1994). These "tertiary characteristics" tend to be the most visible ones to educators and parents. Examples include: poor academic skills, poor organization and study skills, lack of concentration, and behavior problems. A weakness in some skill area or an inability to concentrate or work effectively can make gifted children particularly sensitive and withdrawn. They sense that something is wrong and studiously avoid situations that might expose them to failure.

Causes of Underachievement

Underachievement cannot be said to have any one cause. Some scholars (for example, Delisle 1992; Whitmore 1986) focus on school experiences as the primary cause of underachievement. Gifted children develop underachieving patterns in response to classrooms that routinely deny them the education they need. The lack of support for their talents combined with long periods of boredom prompt them to withdraw from the school experience; they become despondent, resistant to the teacher, and apply themselves as little as possible in school. A number of gifted underachievers fit this description, especially in highly gifted or creative students whose thinking processes depart so radically from the rest of the class that they cannot "fit in" even if they try.

Other researchers argue that gifted children who underachieve often receive reinforcement from sources other than the school, such as family and peer relationships (Rimm 1995). Underachievement also may be tied to learning preferences that create uneven performance in school (Redding 1990) or from social pressures or prejudices that encourage a gifted child from a minority culture not to achieve (Baldwin 2003). Getting at the source of a child's underachievement and the forces in his or her daily life that reinforce it will provide a foundation for creating real solutions to the problem.

Promising Approaches to Improving Achievement

There are a number of promising approaches to improving the achievement of underachieving gifted students. None of these is radical, but each merits specific attention in order to be successful.

Begin with the Individual. Underachievement covers a broad spectrum of situations. One case might be a child who has a minor motivation problem with a fairly obvious cause, while another has underachieved all of his or her years in school for reasons that are not immediately clear. Because underachievement is a varied and complex phenomenon, each case must be examined with the sense that there is no other quite like it. Hansford (2003) observes: "Underachievement is very specific to the individual child; intervention and remediation of underachievement must be individually developed and implemented" (p. 300).

Rimm's well-known Trifocal Model (1986b, 2003) begins with a thorough assessment of the child's intelligence, creativity, and areas of achievement, as well as underachieving behaviors. This kind of assessment provides a detailed picture of the child's gifts, interests, and feelings about school and the areas of his or her life that need to be addressed. Teachers or counselors working with an underachiever will need to consult a range of sources: test scores, performance in school, performance outside of school, and interests and self-directed pursuits. They will need to gather observations from parents, club leaders, and community center activity directors and talk to the student directly. The more sources they have, the better. As already mentioned, under-achievers' abilities may or may not show up in standardized tests. Some have an exceptional verbal ability, expressing complex thinking in eloquent and articulate ways. Yet when it comes to writing, they become perfectionistic and tense, barely getting down a few sentences.

Create Teacher-Parent Collaboration. Even in cases where children are underachieving primarily because of a difficult school environment, parents can significantly advance any improvements designed by the teacher. Without parent involvement, teachers operate in a vacuum and may have little or no support at home for efforts they are making in the classroom. The most successful interventions involve parent-teacher collaborations (see, for example, Rimm 1986b, Heacox 1991, Fine and Pitts 1980), through which the significant adults in a child's life coordinate their efforts and design an effective program for reversing under-achievement. Some of the questions teachers and parents can explore together include:

In what areas has the child shown exceptional ability?

What are her preferred learning styles?

What insights do parents and teachers have about her strengths and problem areas?

What does the child say about her needs, interests, and school experiences and how is this information to be interpreted?

What external factors might be influencing her performance in school — culture, bilingualism, gender, family history?

What factors in school — lack of intellectual challenge, social isolation, difference in learning style and thinking — could cause this withdrawal from school and learning?

This kind of joint exploration can yield useful insight into the nature of the child's abilities and potential causes of under-achievement. Teachers or parents may not fully understand the nature of the child's gifts, they may blame nonachievement on laziness or obstinacy, or they may feel sorry for the child and misattribute his or her difficulties. Some researchers view school and family factors as complex, interactive systems in which actions in one cause reactions in the other (Peterson 2003). By meeting with each other, both teachers and parents can begin to resolve misunderstandings about the student; his or her relation-ships with family, peers, and teachers; and the underachieving behaviors.

Meetings between teachers and parents should uncover specific causes of underachievement as well as contributing factors. These causes might include: unproductive family dynamics or events, ineffective or negative family responses to a child's rebelliousness or apathy, distractions that the child uses to avoid anxiety, negative or inappropriate attitudes about the child from other family members, school activities the child finds difficult or uncomfortable, actions by the teacher about which the student regularly complains, and problems the child has with peer relationships. If teachers and parents familiarize themselves with the characteristics of gifted underachievers and the kinds of avoidance behaviors under-achieveing students use to distance themselves from failure, this will help them discover where the family or the teacher may be reinforcing the problem.

Establish High Expectations. Children often fulfill the prophe-cies — spoken or unspoken — that adults hold about them. Bloom (1985) found that high-achieving parents expect their children to do well in school and, generally, they do. At the same time, however, parents who are personally invested in their child's success and who "live through" the child, may unwitting-ly sow seeds of underachievement (Peterson 2003). Parents and teachers need to take the pressure off a gifted child struggling to meet adult expectations and help the student focus on what he or she would like to do. What goals will give the student the "breath-ing space" to use his or her talents?

In cases where adult expectations for a student are low, teachers and parents need to be able to say honestly that they know the student *can* achieve (Davis and Rimm 1994) and then help the student set realistic goals. Teachers and parents should help the child focus on his or her gifts and design a system that enables the student to experience and explore his or her own strengths. So doing builds the confidence the child needs to manage problem areas and persevere. When a gifted student "owns" his or her abilities, the student will feel less incapacitated by the tasks that pose a challenge.

Agree on Accountability. Rimm's Trifocal Model (1995, 2003) operates on the philosophy that underachievement is learned and, therefore, achievement also can be learned. One of the strategies used to ensure that learning takes place is the creation of accountabilities for the teacher, parents, and child (see also, Fine and Pitts 1980). Children who have underachieved for a long time especially need clear goals and responsibilities to prevent periodic setbacks. The solution for each child involves specific support for abilities and a series of adjustments in school and at home that address skill deficiencies, poor work habits, or other problems.

For example, a creative student might have underachieved for most of her elementary school years. Her father indulges her because he also had problems in school, and he blames the teacher and curriculum. As her grades continue to drop below average, the child develops a low self-esteem, which her mother reinforces by blaming the girl for poor performance and sloppy work habits. The child's organizational skills worsen, and she begins to fall seriously behind in some subjects. The child's struggle to achieve is rooted partly in a school that offers little stimulation for creative students and partly in parents who do not agree on how to cope with her falling grades.

To reverse this student's underachievement, the teacher and both parents need to come to a specific agreement about adjustments that each needs to make. For example, the teacher may agree to provide more opportunities for the child to exercise her creative gifts. In exchange the child agrees to apply herself more in skill areas where she is weak. Both parents need to understand that their responses to their daughter reinforce her underachievement (see Rimm 2003). Both the parents and the teacher should agree on specific plans for remediating the child's skills and study habits and for adjusting school and home environments to support her progress. An emphasis on the role of effort in learning (McNabb 1997) and how it increases knowledge and skill development helps the child apply herself in areas she once avoided.

By taking these steps, the child gains clear and uniform expectations from both parents and a teacher who will provide creative alternatives to some of her class work. She understands what her accountabilities are and, with proper reinforcement and support at school and in the home, she can begin to take charge of her own learning (see Delisle 1992). Most cases of underachievement take some time to be solved and require continuous review. As new circumstances and challenges arise, the child may need some changes made in the area of accountabilities or in the reinforcement she gets at home or in school.

Accommodate Creative Learning Styles. In the case just described, a difference in learning style played a part in the child's underachievement. Creative children have a tendency to underachieve because their thinking style diverges significantly from the convergent style rewarded by schools (Peterson 2003). Janos and Robinson (1985) state that schools "tend to reward the less original students and may, indeed, exacerbate the problems of some creative children" (p. 182). Avoiding competition (Rimm 1986b) and acceleration, these underachievers often improve once they find themselves in classes where they can exercise their creative powers. Without intervention, these children will begin to experience their unique learning style as a liability or deficiency, rather than a difference.

Creative students need solutions that give them both the freedom to create and training in skill and organization areas where they are weak. Baum, Renzulli, and Hebert (1995) used Renzulli's Type III enrichment to design an intervention model that addresses the creative needs of gifted underachievers and helps them complete projects in a systematic way. In this model, teachers can address individual needs — whether they are limited skills, poor goal-making, or trouble with sequential tasks — without making the child's weaknesses the primary focus or limiting the kind of work the student can do. Research bears out that underachievers — particularly those whose problems are school-based — improve when they have a differentiated curriculum that incorporates a variety of learning styles and a supportive teacher who values learning over performance (Emerick 1992; Dweck,1986).

Address Specific Deficiencies. Rimm (1994) says that skill deficiencies almost always are part of the underachiever's experience because of poor study habits and difficulty paying attention. Most underachievers prefer conceptual tasks to analytical, procedural ones and need special tutoring in study skills, detail analysis, and convergent problem-solving (Redding 1990). The more they understand the unique nature of their gifts and learning styles and the skills they need to ensure their progress in school, the more motivated they will be to apply themselves. Because they are gifted, these students tend to make progress quickly — provided the activities and assignments help them see the relationship between effort and achievement.

Disadvantaged and culturally different children are at particular risk of underachieving (see Chapter Seven) and need the kind of model that Baum and colleagues (1995) designed. A Native American child, for example, who has weaknesses in certain knowledge and skill areas because of poverty and inadequate schooling needs an individualized program that focuses on mentoring in the development of his or her gifts and provides special intervention to strengthen skills. Research on culturally different and disadvantaged gifted students has produced a number of effective models (Smutny 2001) that educators can use to help reverse underachievement. These models show 1) how factors such as cultural difference, prejudice, peer pressures, and impoverishment lead to underachievement and 2) the kinds of programs that help children overcome barriers to achievement and success.

The Importance of Advocacy

Gifted students who struggle in school need at least one significant adult in their lives to be their advocate (Smutny 2003).
The active involvement of mentors or role models with whom the
children can identify and in whom they can confide when they
face obstacles is a critical component of any solution for gifted
underachievers (Rimm 1986b; 2003). This advocate could be a
parent, a teacher, a tutor, a relative, or someone in the community who recognizes the children's talents and intervenes on their
behalf. Children who feel inadequate have a particularly difficult
time sustaining their interest and motivation when a challenging
task makes them aware of some weakness they have in skill or
knowledge areas. A mentor advocate can remind them of their
strengths and abilities when they feel overwhelmed, guide them
to take practical steps to develop their skills, and help them deal
with their anxieties and sensitivities over the expectations and
opinions of others.

Underachievers who have reversed their underachievement
invariably credit someone who played an instrumental part in
their freedom. Emerick (1992) cites the special characteristics of
teachers who have helped underachieving gifted students turn
their lives around:

- real affection and interest in the children's lives,
- an affinity with the students that makes communication
  easy,
- a sensitivity that enables teachers to establish reasonable
  goals and expectations for the children,
- an enthusiasm for the students' interests and talents, and
- an ability to develop these talents through varied teaching
  strategies.

The children I have seen emerge successfully from difficult
school experiences have been those who had a special person in
their lives, someone who was committed to their success when
they were not, who cared for them when they felt alone or inad-

equate, who supported them through all their doubts and fears. The support, affection, encouragement, and wisdom that true advocates bring to their role can change the course of a child's life (Smutny 2001).

Concluding Thoughts

Without greater recognition of the underachievement phenomenon, a large population of highly able students will continue to stagnate in our schools. Children in culturally different and low socioeconomic communities perhaps have experienced the most neglect of all (see Chapter Seven). All of these children stand to benefit from schools that have more information about gifted underachievers, their characteristics, and special needs. All would have a greater chance of reversing their underachievement if students were screened for potential as well as performance and if schools had adequate support structures to ensure children with high potential do not slip through the cracks.

The greatest message that gifted underachievers have to offer the field of education is a reminder that the gifted are not impervious to social and emotional challenges. The myth of self-assured gifted children who have more potential than average students and therefore need less help has blinded some educators to these students' real emotional needs and sensitivities. Because of their abilities, many gifted students experience heightened stresses and pressures — sensitivity to expectations, anxiety over performance, perfectionism, and exaggerated responses to the perceptions of others (Millar and Torrance 2003). To keep these students from losing touch with their potential, teachers and parents need to address the emotional and spiritual well-being of gifted children.

Notes

Baldwin, A.Y. (2003). Lost and found: Achievers in urban schools. In J.F. Smutny (Ed.), *Underserved gifted populations: Responding to their needs and abilities.* (pp. 83-91). Cresskill, N.J.: Hampton.

Baum, S.M.; Owen, S.V.; and Dixon, J. (1991). *To be gifted and learning disabled.* Mansfield Center, Conn.: Creative Learning.

Baum, S.M.; Renzulli, J.S.; and Hebert, T.P. (1995). Reversing under-achievement: Creative productivity as a systematic intervention. *Gifted Child Quarterly,* 39: 224-235.

Bloom, B.S. (Ed.). (1985). *Developing talent in young people.* New York: Ballantine.

Davis, G.A. and Rimm, S.B. (1994). *Education of the gifted and talented.* 3rd ed. Boston: Allyn and Bacon.

Delisle, J.R. (1992). *Guiding the social and emotional development of gifted youth.* White Plains, N.Y.: Longman.

Dweck, C.S. (1986). Motivational processes affecting learning. *American Psychologist* 41: 1040-1048.

Emerick, L.J. (1992). Academic underachievement among the gifted: Students' perceptions of factors that reverse the pattern. *Gifted Child Quarterly* 36: 140-146.

Fine, M.J., and Pitts, R. (1980). Intervention with underachieving gifted children: Rationale and strategies. *Gifted Child Quarterly* 24: 51-55.

Gallagher, J.J. (1985). *Teaching the gifted child.* 3rd ed. Newton, Mass.: Allyn and Bacon.

Hansford, S. (2003). Underachieving gifted children. In J.F. Smutny (Ed.), *Underserved gifted populations: Responding to their needs and abilities.* (pp. 293-306). Cresskill, N.J.: Hampton.

Heacox, D. (1991). *Up from underachievement: How teachers, students, and parents can work together to promote student success.* Minneapolis, MN: Free Spirit.

Janos, P.M., and Robinson, N.M. (1985). Psychosocial development of intellectually gifted children. In F.D. Horowitz and M. O'Brien (Eds.), *The gifted and talented: Developmental perspectives* (pp. 149-95). Washington, D.C.: American Psychological Association.

Marland, S. (1972). *Educating the gifted and talented* (Report to Congress, Section 582). Washington, D.C.: U.S. Government Printing Office.

McNabb, T. (1997). From potential to performance: Motivational issues for gifted students. In N. Colangelo and G.A. Davis (Eds.), *Handbook of gifted education* (pp. 408-15). 2nd ed. Boston: Allyn and Bacon.

Millar, G.W., and Torrance, E.P. (2003). School guidance and counseling for the underserved gifted: Strategies to facilitate the growth of leaders, thinkers, and change agents. In J.F. Smutny (Ed.), *Underserved gifted populations: Responding to their needs and abilities.* (pp. 53-80). Cresskill, N.J.: Hampton.

National Commission on Excellence in Education. (1984). *A nation at risk: The imperative for educational reform.* Washington, D.C.: U.S. Government Printing Office.

Peterson, J.S. (2003). Underachievers: Students who don't perform. In J.F. Smutny (Ed.), *Underserved gifted populations: Responding to their needs and abilities.* (pp. 307-32). Cresskill, N.J.: Hampton.

Peterson, J.S. (1999). Gifted—through whose cultural lens? *Journal for the Education for the Gifted* 22(4): 354-383.

Redding, R.E. (1990). Learning preferences and skill patterns among underachieving gifted adolescents. *Gifted Child Quarterly* 34: 72-75.

Richert, E.S. (1991). Patterns of underachievement among giftred students. In Bireley, M. and Genshaft, J. (Eds.), *Understanding the gifted adolescent: Educational, developmental, and multicultural issues* (pp. 139-162). New York: Teachers College Press.

Rimm, S.B. (2003). Underachievement: A continuing dilemma. In J.F. Smutny (Ed.), *Underserved gifted populations: Responding to their needs and abilities.* (pp. 333-44). Cresskill, N.J.: Hampton.

Rimm, S.B. (1995). *Why bright kids get poor grades.* New York: Crown.

Rimm, S.B. (1988). *AIM-TO: Achievement identification measure — Teacher observation.* Watertown, Wis.: Apple.

Rimm, S.B. (1987). *GAIM: Group achievement identification measure.* Watertown, Wis.: Educational Assessment Service.

Rimm, S.B. (1986). *AIM: Achievement identification measure.* Watertown, Wis.; Educational Assessment Service. *a*

Rimm, S.B. (1986). *Underachievement syndrome: Causes and cures.* Watertown, Wis.: Apple Publishing. *b*

Ross, P. (Ed.). (1993). *National excellence: A case for developing America's talent.* Washington, D.C.: U.S. Government Printing Office.

Smutny, J.F. (2003) *Underserved gifted populations: Responding to their needs and abilities.* Cresskill, N.J.: Hampton.

Smutny, J.F. (2001). *Stand Up for Your Gifted Child.* Minneapolis, Minn.: Free Spirit.

Van Tassel-Baska, J. (1992). *Planning effective curriculum for gifted learners.* Denver, Colo.: Love.

Whitmore, J.R. (1989). Re-examining the concept of underachievement. *Understanding Our Gifted* 2(1): 10-12.

Whitmore, J.R. (1986). Preventing severe underachievement and developing achievement motivation. In J.R. Whitmore (Ed.), *Intellectual giftedness in young children: Recognition and development.* New York: Haworth.

Whitmore, J.R. (1980). *Giftedness, conflict, and underachievement.* Needham Heights, Mass.: Allyn and Bacon.

CHAPTER NINE

Program Planning

There are as many kinds of gifted programs in the United States as there are gifted children, or so it would seem. While many of these programs include similar elements, each one serves a particular community of students, parents, teachers, and administrators. Even programs that operate independent of the school system — through the sponsorship of a local university, for example — still must respond to the often conflicting needs and interests of these groups. How each program meets the education needs of its gifted population while remaining answerable to a wide range of demands is part of the "dance" of creating gifted programs (Smutny 2003).

In this chapter I will explore the most important steps for planning and implementing a viable gifted program. This information comes partly from experts in the field and partly from my personal experience in designing and developing gifted programs over many years.

Planning

Usually a school district appoints a committee or task force with representation from various perspectives — parents, teachers, administrators, counselors, community leaders, and so forth. The main job of this group is to write a plan that will serve as an operational guide for implementing the program. In the case of an independently administered program, such as one within an institute or college, the committee most likely will include a university professor as well. The written plan should address the following areas:

Philosophy
Goals and objectives
Population to be served
Admission criteria
Budget
Program structure and design: acceleration and enrichment
Staffing and staff responsibilities
Facilities, schedules, materials, and supplies
Evaluation

In school-based programs the appointed committee usually includes district and building administrators, a gifted education coordinator, parent and teacher representatives, selected support personnel (librarian or learning center director, school social worker or psychologist), and, if already selected, those teachers who will be directly involved in the gifted program. If the gifted program includes the secondary schools, it may be appropriate to invite a student representative to serve on the committee. The committee should involve persons with diverse experiences and points of view who share a common commitment to gifted education.

The committee may wish to consider hiring a consultant to assist in developing objectives and the program design. State education departments, local universities, and professional organizations in gifted education can recommend qualified consultants. Also, national and state conferences foster networks of parents, teachers, and scholars, which can lead to useful contacts and information on topics in gifted education.

During the planning stage, the committee should establish a timeline for completing its work. A timeline creates a structure and focus for the committee and helps to maintain momentum during the preparations. Some planning groups distribute the workload by asking various members to do the research and make recommendations in particular areas. In other cases, the principal or district staff person, the gifted coordinator, and the consultant assume primary responsibility for research and design. In the latter type of organization, the committee serves as a deliberative body that reviews, critiques, and gives approval for the plan.

A good starting point for any committee is to review existing state guidelines and regulations governing gifted education programs. The committee also might want to visit programs in nearby school districts and perhaps attend a university-sponsored weekend or summer workshop for gifted children to understand how others are conducting gifted programs. Administering a survey is an efficient way of soliciting input from the teaching staff, administrators, parents, and students concerning the proposed program.

Program Philosophy and Goals

The philosophy and goals establish the *who, what, when, where, why,* and *how* of the gifted program. These form the rationale that parents, teachers, administrators, school board members, and funding partners require in order to support and participate in the endeavor. According to the Richardson Foundation study (Cox and Daniel 1985), effective gifted programs usually have a written philosophy and a list of specific goals. The philosophy statement tells readers why the program exists and what kind of program will be offered, based on a district's or school's values and priorities and other local needs.

In creating a philosophy and goals, program developers should consider these questions: What need, situation, circumstance, or observation stimulated the idea for this program? What do gifted children most need in this community? What kind of needs assessment has been done to determine this? What research on giftedness and gifted education might benefit this community? Are there any services for gifted students in this community or district and, if so, do they meet the expectations of the children, parents, administration, and teachers involved? To answer these questions, the planning group will need to decide how to gather this information, whether through questionnaires, interviews, or informal meetings with parent groups, district policy makers, teachers, and university researchers. Certain priorities and needs will surface from this activity, and the planning group will gain a clear picture of how the various constituents envision the program.

For example, the programs that I have developed through the Center for Gifted at National-Louis University in Evanston, Illinois, respond to the creative needs of gifted children from preschool through grade 10. Classes emphasize creative thinking in the arts, sciences, and humanities and offer hands-on activities, such as experiments, art work, inventions, performances, and research projects, which develop students' potential for innovation and discovery. As an independently administered program, the focus on creativity and experimentation gives students an alternative to the work they usually do in the schools.

The goals section of the philosophy statement is usually a shortened version of the written program plan. The goals description includes definitions of "gifted" and "talented," a rationale for the program, screening and identification methods, instructional strategies and curriculum, and program evaluation. Van Tassel-Baska's (1988a) *Comprehensive Curricula for Gifted Learners* and Juntune's (1981, 1986) descriptions of gifted programs across the country provide useful guidance on how to formulate program goals.

Target Population

Early in the planning process the committee must identify the target population to be served by the gifted program. What population does the program seek? All gifted students within certain schools or districts? Academically gifted? Creatively talented? High achievers in math and science? This is a critical point to consider because the target population will determine the criteria used for identification, curriculum development, and assessment. For example, I once developed a program for gifted bilingual students that involved re-evaluating and redesigning selection procedures, hiring bilingual consultants to advise on course content and teaching styles, and developing projects sensitive to the cultural and linguistic differences of gifted bilingual children. The program also required community aides, bilingual teachers to help in classrooms where gifted students needed extra language support, and a system for maintaining regular contact with parents. Target populations should always be identified in the philosophy statement, because their needs and strengths influence the kind of program proposed.

Admission Criteria

After selecting the target population the committee must decide what criteria can assess student ability in the most equitable and comprehensive way. This is a challenging task. Although established federal and state guidelines offer leads, it is important to establish more specific admission criteria to accommodate students who may not appear gifted through conventional measures. Most schools use some form of standardized test as an initial indicator of student ability. However, as discussed in previous chapters, test scores should not be the sole criterion for program nomination, much less admission.

Unless the program is specialized — for example, Julian Stanley's (1991) well-known programs for highly gifted math students — the fairest policy is to use multiple criteria. This can mean any combination of the following: standardized tests, performance in school, teacher observations, parent observations, portfolios of work (from home as well as school), informal interviews, and observations by community members. Ideally, each of these criteria should be equally weighted. In other words, a test score should not count more in a student's favor than an exceptional science or art project or observations of a child's analytical abilities in a field experience. Giving weight to data from several sources provides a statistical profile for each candidate, which helps to make the admission process more comprehensive.

Each planning group must decide what measures of ability are practical and equitable within the limitations of the program. Limited budgets and resources often mean that programs cannot accommodate as many gifted students as they would like. While the criteria chosen need to include other modes than testing, they also have to be defensible. It is important that the admission criteria be spelled out in writing and available to anyone involved or interested in the program.

Having written criteria means that teachers and administrators can refer to them when parents ask, "Why my child?" or, more likely, "Why *not* my child?" Candidates who come close to the cut-off point for admission to the gifted program can be placed on a waiting list and re-evaluated at a later date. Or if the program can accommodate more children, it can adopt a model such as Renzulli's popular Schoolwide Enrichment Model (Renzulli and Reis 1991), in which 15% to 20% of a school becomes part of a "talent pool." Such a model has little need to defend its admission procedures, as students revolve in and out of a resource room to design and implement projects.

Budget

The size and nature of the gifted program will depend heavily on the funding available. The committee will have to consider the budget at every step in the planning process. Davis and Rimm (1994) suggest considering the following expenses when drawing up a budget:

- teacher/coordinator (more than one individual in larger programs),
- physical facilities,
- texts and workbooks,
- special equipment and supplies,
- transportation costs,
- tests and inventories,
- secretarial services,
- office supplies,

- duplicating expenses,
- consultant and inservice training expenses,
- travel to visit other programs,
- travel to state and national conferences,
- services of psychologists and counselors, and
- evaluation expenses (consultant; tests, rating scales, or questionnaires). (p. 56)

When faced with limited funds, the planning group should examine areas in which to cut costs. There may be alternative sources for materials, for example; a few local stores may donate materials for art and science projects. The group also might apply for funds from businesses or agencies that could cover relatively minor costs, such as transportation for gifted students from low socioeconomic backgrounds.

After determining the funds available from the state and those the district has set aside for gifted education, the planning group may still be short of what they need. Independent programs face similar problems. If no extra funds are available in the district or institute, the gifted coordinator or team can explore other options:

Contact a local organization for grant makers. In Chicago, the Donor's Forum provides a vast database of foundations. Two useful websites are: List of Regional Associations of Grant Makers (www.indonors.com/RAGlist.html) and Foundation Center - Links to Philanthropic Resources (http://fdncenter.org/onlib/npr-links/npr05.html). The organizations listed on these websites provide guidance in grant-writing and can help locate potential donors.

Contact foundations for applications and ask for deadline dates.

Write a proposal with a specific project or plan clearly formulated. Most foundations do not want their funds used for operating costs. But they will give money for new dimensions to a program or pay for some aspect of the program that supports the foundation's priorities. For example, I once applied for funding to support the inclusion of minority and urban gifted children who have little or no resources available to them in their communities. Because minority education was central to the foundation's priorities, the Center for Gifted received funds to offer 60 scholarships.

Formulate a strong rationale for your project. Demonstrate real need and clearly explain how the school, district, or organization can fulfill that need based on what it has accomplished so far.

Create a budget that itemizes all costs. Include every anticipated cost for the specific project for which the request is being made. Most application guidelines also request the budget of the sponsoring organization to verify that it is fiscally sound.

Finally, it makes good sense to show the proposal to others before submitting it to a funding source. If possible, it is an excellent strategy to work directly with a grant-making organization for advice and assistance about how best to approach them for funding.

Program Design

In Chapters Three and Four, I explored different approaches and models for accelerating and enriching curricula for gifted students. All that needs to be emphasized here is that in any gifted program, classroom instruction must evolve from higher-level program goals. Renzulli and Reis (1991) point out that a number of programs have gotten into the habit of *entertaining,* rather than educating, gifted students with activities that provide little intellectual or creative substance. Davis and Rimm (1994) offer a useful list of objectives that program designers should keep in mind as they develop short- and long-term curriculum goals:

High achievement; advanced academic skills and content;
Complex, abstract, theoretical thinking;
Creative, critical, evaluative thinking, and other thinking skills;

Scientific research skills;

Library research skills;

Communication (speaking, writing) skills, including creative writing;

Career-related content;

College preparatory content; and

Self-awareness, affective, and humanistic principles. (p. 53)

Related to the concern of turning gifted programs into entertainment is the lack of correlation between program objectives and classroom practices. Van Tassel-Baska (1988b) notes that teachers sometimes develop individual units for a particular group of gifted students that form no link to what other teachers are doing or to the broader goals of a districtwide program. While individual units benefit many students, problems arise when these same students later must repeat what they learned because the program has not developed curriculum from stated goals and objectives. Ideally, curriculum planning and development should extend from kindergarten through high school.

Few districts have time, resources, and personnel to create a comprehensive curriculum for the gifted that has the kind of scope just described. Yet they still can design effective programs that provide a more accelerated and enriched curriculum in each subject area. Research on the parallel curriculum (Tomlinson et al. 2002), differentiated instruction (Tomlinson 1999) and on teaching strategies for gifted children (Winebrenner 1992; Smutny, Walker, and Meckstroth 1997) offer many practical ideas on how regular classroom teachers can adapt their curriculum to the needs of gifted students. These options require inservice training to give teachers the support and mentoring.

Staff Responsibilities

During the early planning stages, program developers need to decide who will be responsible for what. Instituting regular staff meetings is a wise way to begin this process. It creates momentum and helps to solidify the group as a strong working team.

Early meetings could generate a master list of the steps needed to implement the program and establish a timeline. Placing each item on a timeline clarifies priorities and formalizes commitments.

Staff members who assume responsibilities may include teachers on the planning committee, administrative assistants, the budget manager, a counselor, community leaders, and a university consultant. Parents of gifted students also are usually willing to make some of the arrangements, such as ordering materials, supplies, and testing instruments and scheduling bus service. These activities leave the committee free to focus on curriculum development, teacher training, proposal writing, and other priorities.

Support Services and Inservice Training

In addition to teachers and administrative staff, other key individuals may be needed to ensure the success of the program. School counselors and psychologists can interpret test scores and student performance and may be invaluable in assessing the abilities of gifted underachievers. Sometimes they have special areas of expertise (for example, underserved populations, such as learning disabled gifted, bilingual, disadvantaged). If it turns out that school psychologists or counselors have no knowledge about gifted children and do not support the program, the committee may need to hire an outside consultant to fill this role.

As mentioned, most programs need to organize inservice training for staff. It is wise to involve *all* teachers in staff development related to gifted education, whether or not they choose to participate in the program. Teachers who do not participate in the program most likely educate a number of gifted children for part of each day. A well-planned inservice program can provide all teachers with practical strategies for differentiating instruction in the classroom.

Preparing teachers for a program is critical. They have a right and a need to understand the philosophy and goals of the program, the level and type of ability they will most likely encounter among gifted students at the grade level they are teaching, and the problems and issues these children face. When possible, teachers should visit classes in a program, ideally in a related field and at the grade level they will have in their own classes.

Inservice training should reinforce the following qualities:

- advanced level of expertise in an area;
- creativity and imagination;
- use of different learning styles and integration of content areas and media;
- flexibility in dealing with children who are unusually independent or want to attempt out-of-the-way ideas;
- enthusiasm for gifted children and compassion for their unique challenges;
- ability to improvise within projects or activities to create teachable moments that benefit all the students;
- a talent for mentorship — identifying and guiding talent in individual gifted students, especially those who may be struggling in some way; and
- an open attitude about parents and a willingness to communicate and share with them.

Program Evaluation

Evaluation and assessment are discussed in depth in the next chapter. But a brief description here will focus on the essential elements. The first step is to consider who needs to know what. In part, this will depend on the kind of program. Is it a school program? A supplemental program run by a university? An institute? A group of committed parents, teachers, and administrators acting independently?

The second point to consider is the kind of information needed — for whom, and when. Parents, for example, may want to know about the kinds of activities their children did in an advanced math class, and they may want to know this before the program is over. A teacher may want continuous feedback on the projects that the children find the most challenging and why. A program director or board member may want to know at the end of the program what worked (and didn't work) for the participating children. Most critical to the success of any evaluation is ensuring that the process served the program and everyone in it — not that it simply satisfied a requirement.

Evaluation and assessment are both formal and informal, ongoing and final. Most programs need two kinds of evaluation: 1) the day-to-day assessments that alert staff members of areas that need to be addressed right away and 2) the more reflective, thoughtful evaluation that happens after a program is over, when parents, children, and teachers have had a chance to think it all through.

Ongoing evaluation takes place when a gifted coordinator canvasses parents, teachers, or others to see how they feel the program is going. But it need not be this formal. Ongoing assessment also can mean fielding daily questions and concerns from children, parents, support staff, teachers, and administrators. Regular staff meetings also provide a forum for sharing impressions and reports about what is and is not working. Parent seminars (held concurrently with the program) are another venue for the exchange of ideas and information. Parents can discuss the classes and activities that have served their children's needs and interests most effectively. The importance of this kind of informal, daily evaluation cannot be overestimated. Without it, problems that could be avoided linger on and become larger issues by the end of the program.

At the end of the program a more formal evaluation is needed. In the programs that I have developed, teachers evaluate the students on a matrix that lists higher-level thinking and learning behaviors important to that particular class. In addition, they write narrative assessments of the children that provide more details about what the children did well and where they need more work. Parents receive detailed evaluations of their children from each teacher.

Parents and children also evaluate the program. Their perspectives are critical to the continuous improvement and growth of the program. Questionnaires first focus on the program's strengths.

They ask what the children found most beneficial and interesting in the program generally and in specific classes. Parents may also provide detailed information on how they feel the program helped their gifted children and what areas of the program need more attention. What teachers did their children find most responsive and helpful? What activities did their children love doing and why? Did their children feel affirmed, encouraged to try new things, excited about what they were learning?

Building Program Support

Gifted programs cannot survive without support from parents, teachers, administrators, and the community. When budget cuts threaten a program's survival, only the support of these various constituencies can give it a fighting chance. Any program that ignores the sentiments of teachers, overlooks parents who feel their child was unjustly excluded, or neglects to communicate with new board members (who are uninformed about gifted children) is putting itself at risk. The larger community needs assurance that the program is not taking anything away from other students, does not set itself above other programs or people, is serving the real needs of a portion of the district's children, and will work hard to maintain a standard of fairness in the selection of students.

Parents. Information about the program and the selection process should be distributed to every parent, not just to those parents whose children seem to be the most likely candidates. Limiting the information about the program to a selective group is sure to brand the program as "exclusive" and "elitist." When the organizing committee has completed its written plan, the school should schedule an open forum for all interested parents. The written plan should be available for inspection, and plenty of time should be reserved for parents' questions.

When communicating with parents, it is important to explain that there are many types of giftedness and that no single program can address all of these types. It should also be pointed out that although only a small percentage of students will participate directly in the gifted program, elements of the program (for example, creative teaching strategies and curricular innovations) can benefit the entire student body. The person presenting information about the program to parents should be prepared to illustrate several ways in which the gifted program will benefit everyone.

Once the gifted program is under way, information about it can be presented in the context of the district's total education offerings and services. For example, an orientation meeting for parents of kindergartners or for students transferring into the district is a good time to discuss all the school's special educational opportunities, including the gifted program.

The gifted program staff should maintain regular contact with the parents of children participating in the program. Through regular contact, parents develop a better understanding of their child's special educational needs and they become strong advocates for the program. Also, as previously mentioned, parents become more involved as volunteers once they see the benefits of gifted programming for their children.

Community. Community support can help get a gifted program off the ground and, once it is established, protect it when budget cuts threaten. Support can come from a variety of sources, but it must be solicited. More often than not, community support is the result of carefully nurtured relationships requiring a considerable amount of time and energy.

Sources of community support include interested individuals, businesses, civic groups, and social service agencies. The nature of the support will vary. Mentorships, in-kind donations, equipment loans, use of facilities, and contributions of staff time are some options.

One of the best ways of winning community support for gifted programs is through exhibits and performances. These events provide a forum for gifted students to share their best efforts with relatives and friends and offer tangible evidence of the value of the gifted program. Public visibility of the creative talents of gifted children and young people sends a positive message about the quality of the schools and will interest the local economic development office, board of realtors, and other groups that want to attract people and businesses to locate in the community.

Teachers. In building support for the gifted program among teachers, it helps to work with all of the teachers in the system, not just those who will be directly involved. The gifted program staff will most likely be those with special training and experience in the field, but regular classroom teachers also should have a thorough grounding in the theory and practice of gifted education. Nancy Johnson (1987) makes a distinction between a gifted program and gifted education. A gifted program is the responsibility of a few designated people, while gifted education is everyone's responsibility. A comprehensive, well-articulated gifted education program requires the involvement of teachers at all levels.

A series of workshops or inservice sessions led by an outside consultant can provide a general overview of gifted education for all teachers. An informal survey of teachers can determine what topics in gifted education are of most interest to them. Teachers of the gifted themselves can be good agents for developing support for the program among their peers.

Barbara Clark (1988) provides the following suggestions for building support:

Watch for those teachers who are interested in what you are doing, invite them into your room, share your materials and ideas, and ask them for their opinions.

Take every opportunity to let the entire faculty know they are welcome at any time to visit, participate, share ideas, or have their students work with your students.

Discuss what you are doing with the principal and other administrators and invite their participation.

Keep parents informed about your goals and activities and invite their participation.

Do not overlook the custodians and office staff. Both can provide invaluable support; they understand how the school operates and know how to get things done that can never be learned from those "in charge."

Attend workshops, conferences, and university classes on gifted education. There you will meet others who share your interests.

Administrators. Support from principals, the superintendent, and school board members ensures the survival of the gifted program and needs to be cultivated. These persons need to understand the program because they may have to field questions, particularly about the student identification and selection process and program content. The interest and involvement of administrators vary. Some may wish to participate in every phase of the program, including student selection and curriculum development; others take a less active role but want to be kept informed through monthly or quarterly reports. Early and continuing contact with administrators by the gifted teacher or coordinator can pay off when problems arise.

Concluding Thoughts

Gifted education advocates often work hard to build initial support for a new program but underestimate the need for continuing support from parents, teachers, administrators, and the community. Because of its status as a "frill" in the minds of many people, the gifted program will need sustained support. Too often, gifted programs are among the first threatened when a district faces budget cuts. The more parents, teachers, administrators, professors, and community members are able to testify to the efficacy of the gifted program, the better a program's chances for survival.

Notes

Clark, B. (1988). *Growing up gifted.* 3rd ed. Columbus, Ohio: Charles E. Merrill.

Cox, J., and Daniel, N. (1985, March/April). The Richardson survey concludes. *G/C/T*: 33-36.

Davis, G.A., and Rimm, S.B. (1994). *Education of the gifted and talented.* 3rd ed. Boston: Allyn and Bacon.

Johnson, N. (1987). Cluster grouping in the regular classroom. Paper presented at the Sixth Annual Conference of the American Association of Gifted Children. Arlington Heights, Illinois.

Juntune, J.E. (1981). *Successful programs for the gifted and talented.* Washington, D.C.: National Association for Gifted Children.

Juntune, J.E. (1986). *Summer opportunities for the gifted.* Washington, D.C.: National Association for Gifted Children.

Renzulli, J.S., and Reis, S.M. (1991). The schoolwide enrichment model: A comprehensive plan for the development of creative productivity. In N. Colangelo and G.A. Davis (Eds.), *Handbook of gifted education* (pp. 111-41). Needham Heights, Mass.: Allyn and Bacon.

Smutny, J.F. (Ed.). (2003). *Designing and developing programs for gifted students.* Thousand Oaks, Calif.: Corwin.

Smutny, J.F.; Walker, S.Y.; and Meckstroth, E.A. (1997). *Teaching young gifted children in the regular classroom.* Minneapolis, Minn: Free Spirit.

Stanley, J.C. (1991). An academic model for educating the mathematically talented. *Gifted Child Quarterly* 35: 36-42.

Tomlinson, C.A. (1999). *The differentiated classroom: Responding to the needs of all learners.* Alexandria, Va.: Association for Supervision and Curriculum Development.

Tomlinson, C.A., et al. (2002). *The parallel curriculum: A design to develop high potential and challenge high-ability learners.* Thousand Oaks, Calif.: Corwin.

Van Tassel-Baska, J. (1988). *Comprehensive curricula for gifted learners.* Boston: Allyn and Bacon. *a*

Van Tassel-Baska, J. (1988). Developing scope and sequence in curriculum for the gifted learner: A comprehensive approach. Part I. *Gifted Child Today* 11(2): 2-7. *b*

Winebrenner, S. (1992). *Teaching gifted kids in the regular classroom.* Minneapolis, Minn: Free Spirit.

CHAPTER TEN

Program Evaluation

Accountability of gifted programs to those who sponsor or support them should make evaluation a top priority in gifted education. School boards, legislators, parents, funding organizations, and the tax-paying public want to know — and have a right to know — if special school programs are delivering what they promise, and this includes programs for the gifted. However, a lack of direction and a dearth of exemplary practice on a number of assessment issues continue to hamper the efforts of gifted program administrators, teachers, and parents (Callahan 1995).

Evaluating gifted programs presents a number of practical and conceptual challenges (Carter 1992, Southern 1992). Programs tend to focus on compliance with state regulations rather than on program goals or the quality of instruction (see Ross-Fisher 1996). Another difficulty relates to goals and objectives that do not lend themselves to the sort of straightforward assessment that would be possible, for example, in a basic skills program evaluated through achievement tests (Davis and Rimm 1994). Also, because the amount of time children typically spend in the gifted program is limited, it is difficult to distinguish outcomes attributed to the gifted program from those of the regular program. Finally, most gifted education programs today operate on a shoe-string budget and would prefer to spend precious funds on program needs rather than evaluation (Ross-Fisher 1996).

Despite all the hindrances to evaluation, gifted programs that fail to provide for it put themselves at risk. Dettmer (1985) explains: "Because gifted programs are not popular and probably never will be, they must be defended and promoted by solid evidence of gifted student growth, cost effectiveness of the program and positive ripple effects for all students throughout the school system" (p. 146). The challenge is to design a model that responds to the legitimate concerns of those who determine the program's survival but also benefits students, parents, and teachers who may have quite different questions and priorities.

Clark (1988) suggests that the initial questions of any evaluation should be: Who needs to know what? What persons are involved in or responsible for the gifted program and what do these persons need or expect to know from an evaluation?

Evaluation Focus

As must be expected, school board members, district and program administrators, principals, teachers responsible for delivering the program, teachers whose students are affected by the program, parents of students who are admitted to the program, parents of students who are *not* admitted to the program, and the students themselves all have different expectations about what constitutes a "successful" program. These differences, combined with the complexities involved in assessing goals in a gifted program, can result in mixed reviews, with little or no consensus on what is good and valuable or what needs to be revised and improved.

Two basic (and sometimes difficult to resolve) issues in evaluation are: 1) Who is the evaluation for? and 2) What type of data should be gathered about the program? After these two issues are resolved, there are other important questions regarding evaluation methods and reporting formats. Whose opinions and views should be taken most seriously? Who should get the results? Who is the actual beneficiary of the evaluation? Who should interpret the results and make decisions regarding program changes?

In this chapter I describe evaluations that focus on specific stakeholders (students and parents, teachers, administrators). I also describe a model for evaluation that has proven responsive to all stakeholders (Hertzog and Fowler 1999, Callahan 1986), effective assessment methods, and a five-year evaluation model.

Student-Focused Evaluation

The fundamental question all programs must ask themselves is whether they are meeting student needs (Ross-Fisher 1996). An evaluation that focuses on the *clients* — students and parents — will seek to determine the extent to which the program fulfilled its goals and provided services to the benefit of children and their families (Scriven 1980). Such an evaluation addresses the following questions:

Who is the target population? How many are served? What are their ability levels? Is there an equity issue regarding the target population? If so, what is the concern?

What does the program do? Are there adequate services? How is the quality of services perceived by the client? Are the services appropriate to the stated purpose of the program? Are the costs of the program offset by the gains?

How effective is the program? Are gains and growth evident? Are clients satisfied with the program? Is there adequate communication between home and school?

What are the unplanned effects of the program? Are there side effects within the target population? Are there side effects on others not in the program itself? Are there unforeseen problems created by the program?

Scriven's (1980) evaluation plan requires the collection of both "hard" and "soft" data. Hard data on the target population of the program, its size, and characteristics would be followed by collecting information on the actual accomplishment of program objectives. Evaluators would assess this by measuring the gains made by students in the program (through testing, observation forms, rating scales) against a set of criteria of merit and standards. Soft data consist of opinions and reports by students and families of the value of the services they received, feedback by teachers in meetings, and informal discussions.

Practitioner-Focused Evaluation

"Commissioners of evaluations complain that the messages from evaluations are not useful, while evaluators complain that the messages are not used" (Cronbach 1982, p. 29). It can be argued that program evaluations conducted by administrators at the federal, state, or district level have less effect than those implemented by practitioners at the local level. At the very least, teachers need to have a say in evaluation design, because they deliver the program to the students and are in an ideal position to gauge its positive and negative effects.

Davis and Rimm (1994) relate evaluation to what they call a "hierarchy of decision makers." Briefly, this refers to the levels and kinds of information that stakeholders need. Teachers, for example, require more information than either students or parents, who focus primarily on the value of their own experience and the quality of education provided. Teachers assess all of the students' experiences, behaviors, and products in order to evaluate the effectiveness of their instruction and, if necessary, modify educational processes. Most teachers in gifted programs are continually evaluating their classrooms in an informal way — by applying new instructional methods in a subject and analyzing the results, by questioning students on their reasoning and thinking processes, by collaborating with other teachers to explore innovative approaches to group assignments, or by discussing the children's progress with parents.

Believing that practitioners in the field are the key element in program growth and improvement, Cronbach (1982) focuses on other ways to generate new thinking in teachers besides evaluating their own classrooms. Methods he describes include visiting other programs to glean new information and practical knowledge, reading the most current accounts of program development, and attending conference presentations that describe and illustrate innovative practices and program models. As teachers observe or discuss program alternatives, they actively conduct an inner evaluation of their own classrooms in comparison to what they view or read about. Either through interior dialogues or discussion with other practitioners in small informal groups, teachers discuss the new ideas they have seen and heard. They ask themselves:

How does this program really work?
Do I like what I see? Why or why not?
Would it benefit my students? Which elements would work?
What evidence is there to support this approach in our program?
Would the parents of my students support this?
How much work would it be for me?
What's the payoff? Is it worth the extra effort for the students?

If the answers to these queries are fairly positive, the practitioners then proceed to gain information about the practical matters of incorporating or adapting the improvement to fit into their existing programs. They ask:

What needs to happen first?
What will it cost?
What changes need to take place?
What will be the effects?
Whose support do I need to get to make this work?

From this process, teachers can synthesize old and new program elements that are appropriate for their students and that function well within the resources and financial support available and in concert with the interests and values of the community.

Administrator-Focused Evaluation

Another approach to evaluation focuses on program results, primarily for the benefit of administrators (Wholey 1983). The assumption inherent in this model is that because program administrators are held most accountable for the program, they need evidence of its effectiveness in order to make responsible decisions and adjustments from year to year.

To accommodate various points of view in the assessment process, Wholey (1983) recommends an important "pre-evaluation." In this vital first step, the entire administrative and teaching staff discuss program definitions, assumptions, goals, and methods. Such a discussion results in a sense of "ownership" of the program by the staff. As consensus emerges on the priorities of the program, the staff as a whole can establish realistic goals and objectives. The goals that emerge from the pre-evaluation may differ from those originally written by program designers, but they will be goals that everyone understands and supports.

Using his Results-Oriented Management Scale, Wholey suggests the use of the following systematic evaluation scheme in seven steps:

1. Define the program.
2. Agree on the objectives.
3. Agree on a system to assess performance of the objectives.
4. Target acceptable levels of performance.
5. Agree on a system for using information.
6. Gather data on program performance in terms of targets.
7. Communicate program performance to administrator or manager.

The benefit of this type of evaluation is that it ensures greater consistency in program implementation by the various staff members. In programs where administrators and staff do not discuss these issues, where everyone *assumes* an agreement on the written goals and objectives, the actual delivery may be inconsistent or fragmented. A report designed by and for program administrators in consultation with teachers and other staff will document the extent to which they accomplished their goals.

The weakness of this model is that program administrators may learn nothing more than they ask for. The perceptions of students, parents, and teachers do not carry much weight in this scheme. Because of this, Wholey's approach works best for ongoing programs that already have widespread acceptance.

Investigative Evaluation

Some researchers believe that an effective evaluation of a program (or some aspects of a program) should involve outside experts (Guba and Lincoln 1981, Hertzog and Fowler 1999). In this model, the recipient of the evaluation is the general public rather than the client or the program administrators. The model operates on the assumption that taxpayers deserve to know what their tax dollars are buying and that the best way to determine the effects of a program (unintended as well as intended) is to conduct an in-depth investigation.

The evaluator, rather than evaluating the program on its stated goals and objectives, assumes the role of participant-observer to learn about the processes and effects of the program. Every program has a "hidden curriculum" that may have effects and consequences as powerful as the planned curriculum. A trained participant-observer would gain information about the program by conducting interviews, making observations, and reviewing all records. The evaluator would be trying to determine:

How does this program work?
Who gets what services?
What are the problems with this program?
What is the quality of each element of the program?
What are the explanations for what is observed?
What changes should be made in this program?

Ideally, the evaluators also would draw on their expertise in gifted education to evaluate the extent to which the program needs to update or adjust practices in light of more current research (Hertzog and Fowler 1999).

While this model may intend to gain unbiased information, it cannot guarantee objectivity. The observations may be subject to error if observers make judgments prematurely, based on incomplete records, strongly biased interviewees, or other on-site distortions. Any controversial issue would likely attract the most attention from the observer. This is especially true if the program is complex. The best investigative evaluators return to a site repeatedly to get a more comprehensive view of the program than a single visit would allow.

The strength of this model is that it provides data from original rather than secondary sources. It serves the clients' interests as well as the interests of the greater public who are not receiving services from the program. It also can serve program administrators who are open to firsthand observations and the expertise of outside researchers.

Responsive Evaluation

Stake (1975) developed an interactive model that integrates the interests and concerns of all of the stakeholders involved in the program: students, parents, teachers, administrators, university personnel, and others. Though designed more than two decades ago and originally created to evaluate the arts in education, it has proven to be a useful model for gifted programs today (Callahan 1986, Hertzog and Fowler 1999). The benefit of this approach is that it represents the different values held by the various constituents and provides a more holistic evaluation of the curriculum and how the different stakeholders think about it (Kemmis and Stake 1988).

Incorporating these differences into the evaluation links particular assessments to the questions, concerns, and biases of specific stakeholders. In other words, when the Responsive Evaluation Model documents "successes" or "failures" in various areas of the program, it includes the perspectives or values that determine whether something is a success or not. Hertzog and Fowler (1999) implemented the model to assess an early childhood gifted education program. Hertzog designed an evaluation plan and matrix with the different stakeholders' questions, issues or concerns and listed the sources and methods for gathering the data. The process resulted in significant transformations, reflecting more current research on giftedness, identification, and curriculum.

Considering the Evaluation Models

Programs are continually evolving. Some changes come about through carefully planned evaluations, while others are brought about by less formal methods. It is important to consider the use of multiple methodologies, sources, and reporting formats (formal and informal) to evaluate and improve gifted programs (Hunsaker and Callahan 1993). The methods adopted need to provide an accurate representation of the program elements under examination and should answer the question: Does this approach adequately measure the benefits of this particular aspect of the program? For example, gifted students in a mathematics class may not show significant improvement on pre- and post-tests. Yet a review of their projects while *in progress* or their dialogue while solving problems clearly demonstrates growth in mathematical reasoning and original thinking. The problem here may be that the tests simply do not measure the abilities emphasized in this class or it may be that tests cannot adequately capture what both teachers and students accomplish together as they devise new ways to solve math problems.

Both informal and formal methods must respond to the *kind* of evaluation undertaken. Is this assessment an ongoing one in which a teacher wants to know from week to week how well students are achieving so that the teacher can plan future classes accordingly? This *formative* evaluation occurs throughout the program and seeks a constant flow of information that the teacher can put to immediate use. On the other hand, is this a final, end-of-the-program assessment for staff and administrators who want a comprehensive picture of the program's effectiveness? This *summative* evaluation gathers a wide range of data on various aspects of the program and assessments from constituencies (parents, students, teachers, community members). Summative evaluations usually have a broader, more comprehensive focus and seek information that will inform future directions for the program.

Informal Evaluation

Informal evaluations of a program go on every day. Teachers and administrators evaluate options every time they plan a learning event or some new program practice. As they implement their plan, they make alterations because of immediate perceptions of needs; the next time they plan the same event, they make revisions based on the outcome of the first attempt. Informal evaluations can take many forms:

Staff Meetings. In the administration of a program, there is a continual need for events that allow stakeholders to participate in discussions about the program. For example, staff members could meet in a pre-evaluation session before the program begins. Teachers could talk about the goals of the program and engage in discussions about how they envision their classes in light of these goals. Staff meetings frequently are conducted as informal workshops. For programs to continue to be fresh and creative over the years, the process of definition and communication must be an ongoing part of the program — one that consistently informs decision makers about adjustments needed on a daily or weekly basis. Continuous assessment has the welfare of the families and teachers at heart.

Parent and Community Meetings. Community support can make or break a gifted program. Monthly or quarterly meetings of parents and other interested members of the community are designed to elicit ideas, suggestions, and criticisms through informal communication. When parents share their thoughts on a variety of issues, many aspects of the program come to light that give them a more comprehensive view of the circumstances and challenges that administrators, faculty, and staff must face.

At the same time, program staff gain a clearer understanding of parent concerns and become more willing to share *their* issues and challenges. Through such two-way communication, administrators, faculty, and parents can work collaboratively to reach solutions or compromises. These meetings provide critical ongoing assessments that can help teachers and administrators make decisions that respond to the stakeholders.

Even though these meetings are informal, they will be more productive if the convener takes most of the following steps and actively involves other participants:

- Asks two or three persons to take notes.
- Makes announcements.
- Includes a student performance or demonstration.
- Provides an update regarding any concerns voiced at previous meetings.
- Introduces and discusses any parent concerns.
- Introduces and discusses any staff concerns.
- Works on solving problems or addressing concerns.
- Includes time for closing thoughts and comments.

This sort of open format is an essential element in establishing strong two-way communication. Not only does it foster better understanding of and respect for the positions that both staff and parents hold on different issues, but it also creates a greater possibility for collaborative effort.

Journals. Keeping a daily journal or log generates an extraordinary amount of data. Without realizing it, teachers, administrators, and other staff members are constantly evaluating the data in front of them: questions and comments by parents, observations of students, concerns voiced by board members or a funding agency, phone calls from community leaders, behaviors of students as they respond to project ideas, student products, and casual conversations about the activities. The list could go on. Keeping track of this information is an excellent way to fill in the blanks that often occur in more formal evaluations. An ongoing narrative of instructional goals, student responses, parent meetings, and casual observations not only gives the evaluator an immediate perspective on what is and is not working, but it also provides a useful record of program effectiveness from week to week.

Formal Evaluation

Evaluations can be energizing and revitalizing to a program and its staff. Constant examination and discussion of curriculum, student needs, parent concerns, and other issues serve an important function in program improvement, especially in the hands of a dedicated practitioner who is sensitive to the unmet needs of the clientele and the district. But informal evaluations are not sufficient. For many reasons, formal assessment and evidence of change are required. The state and district, for example, require written reports and clear documentation of program outcomes before approving funds for future years. Evaluation demands careful planning, needs assessment, data gathering, interpretation, and recommendations.

Formal evaluation actually begins with the needs assessment. As discussed in the previous chapter, this critical first step informs program designers about the special needs of local gifted populations as well as the interests and priorities of the school community. Data collected in a needs assessment provide a rationale for the kind of program designed and point to elements that require evaluation and assessment.

After a program has been successfully launched, the formal evaluation turns from an assessment of needs to documentation of the effectiveness of the services and learning experiences. For example, program staff must address state guidelines in summative evaluations, if state funding of the program is granted; and the state usually provides forms and directions for the collection of data that they require. Following are some formal evaluation strategies:

Tests. Davis and Rimm (1994) recommend obtaining two measurements, if possible, for each program objective. In some cases, designing tests and rating scales may be the best solution to finding an instrument precise enough to measure changes from pretest to post-test. However, instruments developed to assess gifted programs already exist (for example, Renzulli and Reis 1985 and Feldhusen 1991) and can be adapted to the circumstances and goals of individual programs. Some programs do not test students because of the problems involved in finding suitable instruments or the time and expense required to locate or develop and administer them. Where testing is necessary, program administrators need to ensure that instruments actually measure the element or quantity they intend them to. Otherwise, they may draw erroneous and potentially harmful conclusions about the gains made by students.

Questionnaires. Questionnaires usually include a series of straightforward yes-no or multiple-choice questions that can be rated (for samples, see Davis and Rimm 1994, pp. 433-39). The questionnaires I have developed include anecdotal sections in which respondents can critique aspects of the program in some detail. Most gifted programs use questionnaires to assess student attitudes, parents' perceptions of the program, and teachers' views on their classes and the program's overall performance.

Ratings of Student Products. A source that always should be considered when evaluating any program are student products. Such products can best be considered by collecting individual portfolios of students' work. These portfolios might include art work, research papers or original writing done in an English class, science projects, mathematical proofs, or student-designed computer programs. Student products collected over a period of time, when evaluated with a set of established criteria, provide a record of growth and achievement.

As difficult as it may seem to evaluate products objectively, program evaluators can itemize particular abilities and rank students' work on a scale of one to five. For example, an art class can focus on specific qualities, such as sophistication of design, originality in concept and execution, high-level skill and ease in manipulating different art media, and evidence of analytical thinking in solving art problems.

A Five-Year Evaluation Schedule

A number of important issues and elements must be assessed in a gifted program. To attempt to evaluate everything each year will likely result in only superficial information. Also, if program designers assess too many elements in a single year, they will be unable to act effectively on them all. Much of the information will sit unused in a file cabinet. On the other hand, if they can schedule evaluations of specific program elements on a rotating basis, they can focus their efforts to improve the program in a more effective and systematic way.

A five-year rotation (Eby and Smutny 1990), for example, allows program staff to focus on evaluating one of the five major concerns addressed in the schedule that follows. As the plan suggests, every five years it is important to reconsider and update old decisions. Even the basic questions of philosophy and definitions should be re-examined every five years in light of changes in the community, newly hired personnel, revised board policies, and new research findings.

Following is a sample five-year schedule.

Year 1: Philosophy and Definition Issues
     A. Talent areas to be served
     B. Definition of giftedness or talent in each area

Year 2: Identification Issues
     A. Target population
          1. Numbers served in each talent area
          2. Numbers served at each grade level
          3. Levels of ability or talent required to be admitted
          4. Criteria for selection established or reviewed
          5. Instruments and other procedures reviewed
     B. Identification of equity issues among nontarget population

Year 3: Services
     A. Types
     B. Quantity
     C. Quality
     D. Variety
     E. Relative costs
     F. Satisfaction

Year 4: Curriculum Issues
    A. Acceleration, enrichment, or independent study
    B. Curriculum areas
    C. Curriculum goals and objectives
    D. Appropriateness of instructional strategies
Year 5: Effects
    A. Planned effects for each talent area served
    B. Unplanned effects

During the first year of the evaluation rotation, the administration, faculty, and staff assess the community's agreement with the program philosophy and related questions about the talent areas to serve in the program. Even in a well-established program, these questions may help discover new information about the talents and unmet needs of the students in the district, as well as pertinent research on giftedness. Program designers should act as soon as possible to refine their philosophy statements and reconsider the talent areas they serve based on the information received.

In the second year of the evaluation rotation, the program evaluators conduct needs assessments on identification issues and act on them as required. It is vital to reassess whom the program is serving, and how students are selected. Program staff must gather data that show exactly which children are being served by the program. Are there inequities in the identification procedures? Do children stay in the program or is there a significant dropout rate? Program administrators must carefully consider whether the data are congruent with the program's definition of giftedness.

During the third year, program staff assess the service needs of their clientele. They re-evaluate the types of services offered in the program, the needs of clients, and their perceptions of the services rendered. Are the types of services offered the ones the client wants? Are they offered in sufficient quantity to actually bring about a desired effect? Too often, gifted programs are offered only a few hours per week. Is this adequate? Is it worth the cost? When the staff ask these questions, they may find a wide range of responses, but the information can be put to use in order to better serve clients.

In the fourth year, evaluators reconsider curriculum issues. Are there other programs in the district that duplicate the program's curriculum? Are there gaps still unfilled? Should curricula be better connected to the regular program? A complete rewrite of the curriculum goals and objectives will have the effect of revitalizing the program and giving a renewed sense of ownership and interest in the program to the teachers (especially new teachers) who deliver the program to the students.

In the fifth year, program staff try to uncover any unplanned effects and impacts of their program that may be undermining their best efforts. They examine longitudinal effects. They can collect data from tests, observations, checklists, and product evaluations and use other methods of assessing student performance and growth. How do students in the program compare with those who are not in the program? How do students in one part of the program compare with those in another? During this year, they should also conduct a survey of those outside the program to discover what, if any, unexpected impacts the program has on the school community.

The benefit of this five-year evaluation plan is that each year program designers can plan and carry out a well-organized and complete analysis of one important aspect of their program. This approach works well in programs with limited time and resources. The information provides useful guidance and direction for future improvements. Each year, administrators and faculty target specific program elements and make any adjustments that may be needed. The fifth year leads right back to the beginning. Program evaluators will be prepared in the following year to reexamine the fundamental issues of philosophy and definition.

Concluding Thoughts

The gifted education scene is in constant flux. New federal and state guidelines, new sources of funding, new program models, new research in the area of underserved populations, and the movement for increasing parent involvement all influence gifted education. By having a multiyear evaluation process, educators can ensure that their gifted programs respond to these changes systematically and that they continue to provide the education gifted students need.

Notes

Callahan, C.M. (1986). Asking the right questions: The central issue in evaluating programs for the gifted and talented. *Gifted Child Quarterly* 30: 38-42.

Callahan, C.M. (1995). Evaluating instructional outcomes for gifted students. In J.L. Genshaft, M. Bireley, and C.L. Hollinger (Eds.), *Serving gifted and talented students* (pp. 83-99). Austin, Tex.: Pro-Ed.

Carter, K.R. (1992). A model for evaluating programs for the gifted under non-experimental conditions. *Journal for the Education of the Gifted* 15: 166-183.

Clark, B. (1988). *Growing up gifted.* 3rd ed. Columbus, Ohio: Charles E. Merrill.

Cronbach, L. (1982). *Designing evaluations of educational and social programs*. San Francisco: Jossey-Bass.

Davis, G.A., and Rimm, S.B. (1994). *Education of the gifted and talented.* 3rd ed. Boston: Allyn and Bacon.

Dettmer, P. (1985). Gifted program scope, structure, and evaluation. *Roeper Review* 7(3): 146-152.

Eby, J.W., and Smutny, J.F. (1990). *A thoughtful overview of gifted education.* White Plains, N.Y.: Longman.

Feldhusen, J.F. (1991). Saturday and summer programs. In N. Colangelo and G.A. Davis (Eds.), *Handbook of gifted education* (pp. 197-208). Needham Heights, Mass.: Allyn and Bacon.

Guba, E., and Lincoln, Y. (1981). *Effective evaluation.* San Francisco: Jossey-Bass.

Hertzog, N.B., and Fowler, S.A. (1999). Perspectives: Evaluating an early childhood gifted education program. *Roeper Review* 21(3): 222-27.

Hunsaker, S.L., and Callahan, C.M. (1993). Evaluation of gifted programs: Current practices. *Journal for the Education of the Gifted* 16(2): 190-200.

Kemmis, S., and Stake, R. (1988). *Evaluating curriculum.* Geelong, Victoria, Canada: Deakin University.

Renzulli, J.S., and Reis, S.M. (1985). *The schoolwide enrichment model: A comprehensive plan for educational excellence.* Mansfield Center, Conn.: Creative Learning.

Ross-Fisher, R.L. (1996 January/February). Creating an evaluation plan that's right for your program: Monitoring to ensure needs of gifted students are met. *Gifted Child Today*: 32-33, 49.

Scriven, M. (1980). *The logic of evaluation.* Inverness, Calif.: Edgepress.

Southern, T.W. (1992). Lead us not into temptation: Issues in evaluating the effectiveness of gifted programs. In *Challenges in gifted education: Developing potential and investing in knowledge for the 21st century* (pp. 103-108). (ERIC Document Reproduction Service No. EC 301 131).

Stake, R.E. (1975). *Evaluating the arts in education: A responsive approach.* Columbus, Ohio: Charles E. Merrill.

Wholey, J. (1983). *Evaluation and effective public management.* Boston: Little, Brown.

APPENDICES

Following are five sections containing resources that will be useful to program planners, administrators, and teachers. Appendix A includes membership associations and organizations that can provide information about gifted education. Appendix B lists a variety of useful professional journals and magazines. Appendix C includes publishers and suppliers of materials on gifted education. A number of the sources in these three appendices also have websites; additional websites with gifted education content are listed in Appendix D. Finally, Appendix E lists tests and their suppliers. See Chapter Two for a discussion of these tests.

APPENDIX A
ORGANIZATIONS

Association for the Gifted Council for Exceptional Children
1920 Association Drive
Reston, VA 22091-1589
1-800-486-5773
www.cec.sped.org

Center for Gifted
National-Louis University
2840 Sheridan Road
Evanston, IL 60201-1796
(847) 251-2661

Creative Education Foundation
Torrance Center for Creative Studies
University of Georgia
323 Aderhold Hall
Athens, GA 30602-7146
(706) 542-5104

ERIC Clearinghouse on Disabilities and Gifted Education
1920 Association Drive
Reston, VA 22091-1589
1-800-328-0272

Gifted Child Society, Inc.
190 Rock Road
Glen Rock, NJ 07452-1736
(201) 444-6530
www.gifted.org

Hollingworth Center for Highly Gifted Children
827 Central Avenue, #282
Dover, NH 60093
(207) 655-3767

National Association for Gifted Children (NAGC)
1707 L Street N, Suite 550
Washington, DC 20036
(202) 785-4268
www.nagc.org

National Association of State Boards of Education
277 S. Washington St., Suite 100
Alexandria, VA 22314
(703) 684-4000

National Resource Center for the Gifted and Talented (NRC/GT)
University of Connecticut
2131 Hillside Road, Unit 3007
Storrs, CT 06269-3007
(860) 486-4676
www.ucc.uconn.edu/~wwwgt/nrcgt.html

World Council for Gifted and Talented Children
18401 Hiawatha Street
Northridge, CA 91326
(818) 368-7501
E-mail: worldgt@earthlink.net

APPENDIX B
JOURNALS AND MAGAZINES

Gifted Child Quarterly
1155 15th Street, N.W., Suite 1002
Washington, DC 20005
(202) 785-9268

Gifted Child Today
Prufrock Press
P.O. Box 8813
Waco, TX 76714-8813
1-800-998-2208

Gifted Education Communicator
California Association for the Gifted
15141 Whittier Boulevard, Suite 510
Whittier, CA 90603
(562) 789-9933

Gifted Education Press Quarterly Magazine
10201 Yuma Court
P.O. Box 1586
Manassas, VA 20109
(703) 369-5017

Illinois Council for the Gifted Journal
Illinois Association for Gifted Children (IAGC)
550 Frontage Road
Northfield, IL 60093
(847) 501-6151

Journal of the Gifted and Talented Education Council of the Alberta Teachers' Association
Alberta Teachers' Association
Barnett House
11010 142 Street, N.W.
Edmonton, AB T5N 2R1
CANADA

Journal of Secondary Gifted Education
Prufrock Press
P.O. Box 8813
Waco, TX 76714-8813
1-800-998-2208

Roeper Review
Roeper School
P.O. Box 329
Bloomfield Hills, MI 48303-0329
(248) 203-7321

Tempo
Texas Association for the Gifted and Talented
406 East 11th Street, Suite 310
Austin, TX 78701-2617
(512) 499-8248

Understanding Our Gifted
Open Space Communications, Inc.
P.O. Box 18268
Boulder, CO 80308-8268
1-800-494-6178

APPENDIX C
PUBLISHERS AND SUPPLIERS

Alarion Press
P.O. Box 1882
Boulder, CO 80306-1882
1-800-523-9177
www.alarion.com

Offers high-quality books and materials (video packages, wall posters, time lines, lesson plans, reproducible workbooks, activities, computer programs) in social studies, art education, multicultural studies, humanities, gifted and talented, and more. Appropriate from kindergarten through adult.

Bluestocking Press
P.O. Box 2030, Dept. 2
Shingle Springs, CA 95682-2030
1-800-959-8586
www.BluestockingPress.com

Publishes a rich variety of history books (including the "Uncle Eric" books by Richard J. Maybury) and materials that will foster in young minds a lifelong interest in history. The press's goal is to present history in such a way that it encourages critical thinking, reasoning, and responsibility.

A.W. Peller
Bright Ideas for the Gifted and Talented Catalog
210 Sixth Avenue, P.O. Box 106
Hawthorne, NJ 07507
1-800-451-7450
www.awpeller.com

Distributes materials for more than 100 education publishers, producers, and manufacturers. Products include books, kits, videos, posters, games, and CD-ROMs for gifted students K-12.

California Association for the Gifted
5777 West Century Boulevard, Suite 1670
Los Angeles, CA 90045
(310) 215-1832
www.cagifted.org

Offers conferences for educators and families. Publishes the national journal, *Gifted Education Communicator*, featuring articles by leaders in the field, parent-to-parent articles, and hands-on curriculum.

Cobblestone Publishing Company
30 Grove Street, Suite C
Peterborough, NH 03458
1-800-821-0115
www.cobblestonepub.com

Publishes high-quality nonfiction magazines for young readers. Uses the expertise of editors, writers, and advisors in a variety of fields to produce magazines on history, world cultures, science and other subjects in an interesting and engaging way.

Creative Learning Press
P.O. Box 320
Mansfeld Center, CT 06250
(860) 429-8118
www.creativelearningpress.com

Provides a variety of manuals and activity books for teachers working with gifted children, including Renzulli and Reis' best-selling *Schoolwide Enrichment Model* and Reis' *Work Left Undone: Choices and Compromises of Talented Females*. Offers an extraordinary Mentors-in-Print section with a wide range of stimulating, hands-on, how-to books for gifted children at all grade levels.

Creative Teaching Press
15342 Graham Street
Huntington Beach, CA 92649
1-800-287-8879
www.creativeteaching.com

Offers high-quality, innovative and fairly priced products for creative teaching. The materials (everything from books to puppets) cover a broad range of subjects and provide teachers with activity ideas and catalysts for stimulating the imagination and creative thinking in students.

Critical Thinking Books and Software
P.O. Box 448
Pacific Grove, CA 93950
1-800-458-4849
www.criticalthinking.com

Supplies the largest selection of high-quality critical thinking products for kindergarten to adult education. Products aim to improve performance, encourage students at all ability levels, and extend achievement and success.

Dandy Lion Publications
3563 Sueldo, Suite L
San Luis Obispo, CA 93401
1-800-776-8032
www.dandylionbooks.com

Publishes teaching materials that stress development of creative and critical thinking for students in grades K-8. Presents innovative methods for teaching all subjects. Ideal for teachers in gifted and talented programs, teachers in regular classrooms, homeschoolers, and parents.

Free Spirit Publishing Inc.
400 First Avenue North, Suite 616
Minneapolis, MN 55401-1730
1-800-735-7323
www.freespirit.com

Award-winning publisher of nonfiction resources for children and teens, parents, educators, and counselors. Develops a variety of research-based and user-friendly materials on topics such as self-esteem and self-awareness, stress management, school success, creativity, friends and family, peacemaking, social action, and special needs.

Gifted Education Press
10201 Yuma Court
P.O. Box 1586
Manassas, VA 20109
(703) 369-5017
www.cais.com/gep

Publishes books and periodicals on educating gifted children. Extraordinary range of innovative materials for teachers, parents, homeschoolers, and students on all subjects at all grade levels. Press distributes materials in school districts across the nation.

Gifted Psychology Press
P.O. Box 5057
Scottsdale, AZ 85261
(602) 368-7862
www.giftedpsychologypress.com

Publishes books for parents, teachers, counselors, and educators of gifted and talented children. Focuses on subjects such as guiding gifted students, creativity, college planning, self-esteem, legal issues, girls, mentorship, parent advice, and more.

Illinois Association for Gifted Children (IAGC)
550 Frontage Road
Northfield, IL 60093
(847) 501-6151
www.iagcgifted.org

Provides yearly conventions on gifted education. Publishes a journal that features articles on specific topics such as, underserved populations, young gifted children, and teaching strategies for gifted students in the regular classroom.

National Women's History Project
7738 Bell Road
Windsor, CA 95492-8518
1-800-691-8888
E-mail: NWHP@aol.com
www.nwhp.org

Nationally known clearinghouse that provides information and training in multicultural women's history for educators, community organizations, and parents. Aims to recognize and celebrate women's contributions, and insert this record into history. Has an extraordinary range of materials and offers training and teacher support.

New Forum Publishers, Inc.
555 North Lane, Suite 6040
Conshohocken, PA 19428
(877) 946-4622
www.beyondbooks.com

An electronic publisher that recently founded a new division called Beyond Books, an outstanding online source that complements curriculum from grades 6 to 12. Ideal for gifted students as it greatly expands on the regular curriculum, enabling both teachers and students to research more deeply into subjects of interest.

New Moon: The Magazine for Girls and Their Dreams
P.O. Box 3587
Duluth, MN 55803-3587
(218) 728-5507
www.newmoon.org

Publishes magazines for girls. Also offers curricula and learning activities for all grades that correspond with each issue of New Moon. Invaluable resource for teachers, homeschoolers, and girls' group leaders.

Open Space Communications, Inc.
P.O. Box 18268
Boulder, CO 80308-8268
1-800-494-6178
www.openspacecomm.com

Produces a range of books and tapes for those who work and/or live with gifted children. Also publishes the outstanding journal for teachers and parents, *Understanding Our Gifted*.

Pieces of Learning
Division of Creative Learning Consultants, Inc.
1610 Brook Lynn Drive
Beavercreek, OH 45432-1906
1-800-729-5137
www.piecesoflearning.com

Publishes and produces K-12 supplementary enrichment activity books on language arts, resource books, and parenting and staff development videos. Topic areas include critical and creative thinking, questioning skills, and materials for subjects such as language arts, math, writing, literature, thematic learning, research, and much more.

Prufrock Press
P.O. Box 8813
Waco, TX 76714-8813
1-800-998-2208
www.prufrock.com

Publishes innovative products and materials supporting the education of gifted and talented children. Offers teachers and parents of gifted children a comprehensive online education resource. Comprehensive listing of gifted children links and products, gifted education magazines (*Gifted Child Today*), research journals, identification instruments, books and more.

Royal Fireworks Publishing Company
First Avenue, P.O. Box 399
Unionville, NY 10988-0399
(845) 726-4444

Publishes an extensive selection of educational sources — from textbooks on different subjects (all grade levels) to workbooks, fiction, and other materials.

Skipping Stones: A Multicultural Children's Magazine
P.O. Box 3939
Eugene, OR 97403-0939
(541) 342-4956
www.treelink.com/skipping/main.htm

Nonprofit children's magazine that encourages cooperation, creativity and celebration of cultural and environmental richness. Provides a forum for sharing ideas and experiences among children from different lands and backgrounds. An award-winning resource for multi-cultural and global education.

Texas Association for the Gifted and Talented
406 East 11th Street, Suite 310
Austin, TX 78701-2617
(512) 499-8248
www.txgifted.org

Provides yearly convention for teachers, administrators, and parents. Publishes journal on gifted education, *Tempo*, four times a year with articles on a variety of themes, such as leadership, identification, and homeschooling.

Thinking Caps
P.O. Box 26239
Phoenix, AZ 85068
(602) 870-1527

Publishes educational materials for the gifted. Although primarily designed for teachers, parents can use this source to supplement their children's education. Materials based on Bloom's taxonomy.

Thinking Works
P.O. Box 468
St. Augustine, FL 32085-0468
1-800-633-3742

Distributes educational materials from a variety of publishers. Extensive selection useful to both teachers and parents.

Tin Man Press
(Publisher of *Tin Man Times*)
P.O. Box 219
Stanwood, WA 98292
1-800-676-0459
www.tinmanpress.com

Publishes original thinking-skills materials for the elementary grades. Applicable for a broad range of enrichment applications and in gifted programs. Particularly useful for inventive thinkers.

Zephyr Press
Box 66006
Tucson, AZ 85728-6006
(520) 322-5090
zephyrpress.com

Publishes educational materials focusing on multiple intelligences theory. Activities within products integrate disciplines so that the learning is more meaningful. Designed for educators or parents, tools are practical, easy to use, and incorporate latest research.

APPENDIX D
ADDITIONAL WEBSITES

ERIC Digests on Gifted
ericec.org/digests/prodfly.html

Gifted Resources
www.eskimo.com/~user

Gifted Psychology Press newsletter
www.giftedpsychologypress.com

A Glossary of Gifted Education
members.aol.com/svennord/ed/GiftedGlossary.htm

GT World! A Meeting Place for Families and Friends of the
Gifted and Talented
www.gtworld.org

Hoagies' Gifted Education Page
www.hoagiesgifted.org

The Lifeline to the Net's Gifted Resources Index
members.aol.com/discanner/index.html

National Foundation for Gifted and Creative Children
www.nfgcc.org/index.html

National Research Center on the Gifted and Talented
www.ucc.uconn.edu/~wwwgt/nrcgt.html

State Resources for Gifted Education
www.cec.sped.org/ab/federation.html

Suggestions for Surfing the Net with Kids
www.surfnetkids.com

Talent Development Resources
members.aol.com/douglaseby/tdr.html

APPENDIX E
TESTS

Individual Intelligence Tests

Revised Stanford-Binet Test of Intelligence Form LM
Riverside Publishing Company, 1972

Stanford-Binet, Fourth Edition
Riverside Publishing Company, 1986

Wechsler Intelligence Scales for Children – Revised
Psychological Corporation, 1974

Group Intelligence Tests

Cognitive Abilities Test (CogAT)
Riverside Publishing Company, 1954-83

SRA Primary Mental Abilities Tests
Science Research Associates, 1962

Otis-Lennon Mental Ability Test (OLSAT)
Psychological Corporation, 1977-82

Raven Standard Progressive Matrices
Psychological Corporation, 1998

Achievement Tests

Iowa Tests of Basic Skills (ITBS)
Riverside Publishing Company, 1978

Purdue Academic Rating Scales
In Feldhusen, J.F.; Hoover, S.M.; and Sayler, M.F. (1990).
  *Identifying and educating gifted students at the secondary
  level.* Unionville, N.Y.: Trillium.

Stanford Achievement Test
Psychological Corporation, 1973

Metropolitan Achievement Tests (MAT)
Psychological Corporation, 1978

Science Research Associates Achievement Test (SRA)
Science Research Associates, 1978

Creativity Tests

Torrance Tests of Creative Thinking
Scholastic Testing Press, 1974

ABOUT THE AUTHOR

Joan Franklin Smutny is founder and director of the Center for Gifted at National-Louis University. The center offers programs to more than 3,000 gifted children, age four through grade 10, each year. Smutny also teaches graduate courses in gifted education for the university. Through the center's program, she teaches creative writing to children and offers parent seminars and teacher inservice education programs nationally. Smutny also lectures regularly at state and national conferences, focusing on topics such as preprimary and primary education, creativity, curriculum, multiculturalism, gifted girls, the role of the arts, and parent advocacy.

Smutny serves as membership chair for the National Association for Gifted Children. She also is the editor of the *Illinois Association for Gifted Children Journal*, assistant editor of *Understanding Our Gifted*, and a contributing editor for *Roeper Review*. She served as series editor for the creativity division of Ablex Publishing Company and currently is on the editorial board of *Gifted Education Quarterly*.

Smutny has written extensively in the field of gifted education. Among her recent publications are *Teaching Young Gifted Children in the Regular Classroom* (1997), *The Young Gifted Child, an Anthology* (1998), *Stand Up for Your Gifted Child* (2001), *Underserved Gifted Populations* (2003), and *Designing and Developing Programs for Gifted Children* (2003). She also is the author of two Phi Delta Kappa fastbacks, 427 *Gifted Girls* (1998) and 506 *Differentiated Instruction in the K-5 Classroom* (2003).

In 1996 Joan Franklin Smutny received the National Association for Gifted Children Distinguished Service Award for outstanding contribution to the field of gifted education.